Praise for *Do Childfree People Have Better Sex*

"Brunschweiger's feminist engagement is as instructive as it's entertaining."—**Susanne Baller**, Journalist, Stern

"The book *Kinderfrei statt kinderlos. Ein Manifest* by the medievalist Verena Brunschweiger is one of the most important publications criticizing society. Reading it is an enjoyment. It brings radical feminism back to the standard of the 1970s and shows who is most interested in pro-natalism: the state and capitalism."—**Dr. Clemens Heni**, Director, Berlin International Center for the Study of Antisemitism

"Brunschweiger's theses are important and worth pondering. They hurt, because they show that having kids is not only an individual decision, but has influence on the fate of every living creature."
—**Marlen Hobrack**, Journalist, Der Freitag

"What if instead of giving birth to children, more women chose to give birth to important ideas and projects, revolutionary inventions, inspiring art, or simply a fulfilling existence? Verena Brunschweiger passionately challenges patriarchal norms, discussing that there is obviously a wider range of roles women can play other than motherhood. But that's not all—she explains how lower birth rates can better the world."—**Dr. Camila Perussello**, Author of *Food for Thought*

"Verena Brunschweiger doesn't want mankind to go extinct. On the contrary, she wants to make sure that there is a future, for people and in general. She tackles a taboo many environmentalists shy away from:

the fact that reducing plastic doesn't suffice if the population growth continues like this. It's her merit to have brought this emotionally and politically difficult topic to everyone's attention. The voluntary renunciation to procreate she propagates is based on ecological reasons. She presents these convincingly in the first part of her book, adding ethical and feminist points."—**Sacha Rufer**, Book Reviewer, Umweltnetz-Schweiz

"I reviewed this delightfully thorough manuscript on the week in which results from a Pew Research Center survey were published, making the front pages of top US newspapers. The survey revealed that the number of US adults of childbearing age saying they are 'not too likely' to have children is on the rise and is now at 21% as compared to 16% in 2018. The more surprising result was the most common reason given: They just don't want them.

"Ms. Brunschweiger's new book pushes back on the concept that not wanting to be a parent is somehow a character flaw, a psychological disorder that can often be cured by having a 'childless' individual spend time around adoring little ones. Her frequent use of the term 'childfree' provides a refreshing read for non-parents, especially given the media's continued insistence on referring to us as 'childless.' Ms. Brunschweiger argues that not only do we have better things to do, we also can feel good about not contributing to an overpopulated planet.

"The book is a must-read for childfree adults from all over the world, a comforting reminder that we share so many experiences, including: a) Being misunderstood, shunned, and demeaned for our choice; b) the vital experiences that result in having more time for living our lives, time for pleasure as well as for giving to our communities; c) being able to take comfort in the fact that we are contributing to saving the world in the only way that might truly make a difference."—**Ellen L. Walker, PhD**, Author of *Complete Without Kids*

"Apart from the philosophical approach of anti-natalism she explains the advantages of a childfree relationship, in which other aspects than organizational ones are in the focus."—**Claudia Wangerin**, Journalist, junge Welt

Do Childfree People Have Better Sex?

A Feminist's Journey in the Childfree Movement

Verena Brunschweiger, PhD

Lantern Publishing & Media ● Brooklyn, NY

2022
Lantern Publishing & Media
128 Second Place
Brooklyn, NY 11231
www.lanternpm.org

Copyediting by Pauline Lafosse.
Cover design by Rebecca Moore.

Printed in the United States of America

Library of Congress Cataloging-in-Publication Data

Names: Brunschweiger, Verena, 1980- author.
Title: Do childfree people have better sex? : a feminist's journey in the childfree
    movement / Verena Brunschweiger.
Description: Brooklyn, NY : Lantern Publishing & Media, [2021] | Includes
    bibliographical references
Identifiers: LCCN 2021049115 (print) | LCCN 2021049116 (ebook) | ISBN
    9781590566640 (paperback) | ISBN 9781590566657 (epub)
Subjects: LCSH: Childfree choice. | Sexual intercourse.
Classification: LCC HQ755.8 .B778 2021 (print) | LCC HQ755.8 (ebook) | DDC
    306.87—dc23/eng/20211013
LC record available at https://lccn.loc.gov/2021049115
LC ebook record available at https://lccn.loc.gov/2021049116

ACKNOWLEDGMENTS

I would like to thank the people whose encouragement has helped make this book possible. One group consists of supporters all around the world, whose kind words kept me going.

Throughout writing, conversations have inspired me and widened my perspective. Thanks in particular to Andrea, Franziska, Marina, Michael, Ruslan, and Thomas.

Special thanks go to the team at Lantern: Brian Normoyle, Pauline Lafosse, Liza Barkova, Emily Lavieri-Scull, Rebecca Moore, and Martin Rowe.

I'm also highly indebted to some great feminists and writers, whose work inspired me immensely: Janice Raymond, Andrea Dworkin, Rita Mae Brown, Sheila Jeffreys, and Gloria Steinem.

Patricia MacCormack wrote a wonderful introduction—thank you so much!

I'm also grateful to my dad and to my one great love. Thanks for your love, support, and consistency.

Contents

About the Author
About the Publisher

INTRODUCTION

Patricia MacCormack

Philosophy, its pre-Reformation inextricability from religion, as well as many scientific fields, strain to respond to two persistent questions: What is the meaning of existence, and why are we here? These are questions driven by the anthropocentric hubris that has decimated the world, affirming a dominating dialectic that Earth exists for humans rather than the reverse or a symbiotic reciprocity. The questions are more correctly posed thus: we exist and believe we are supreme so knowledge must confirm motive, and we want to believe being here matters because humans are special so we will attempt to prove it. Both questions point to a superstition at best beneath our drives to affirm existence as purposeful.

Further relations of equivalence resonate with humans and Earth; as humans exist to dominate and scourge the earth, so men exist to dominate and scourge women, humans exploit and murder nonhuman animals, heteronormativity exists to deny the infinite fluidity and sublime cosmos of queer desire, colonialism and its collaborator neo-capitalism pillage to deny individual value in simply existing, of any and all lives in myriad diversity. What this comes down to is, at the heart of human existence there is a cold fear that there is no value or inherent benevolence in people. Let's face it, our track record is bad and getting worse.

There is a third persistent question, or rather fact, that overshadows all others: Death. Religion offers an afterlife, science

1

offers life extension, transhumanism offers potential eternity albeit in digital form. And, of course, the most common (in every sense of the word) attempt at eternity comes in the form of reproducing. Where legacies of art, literature, and ethics continue to enrich the world, we are currently heaving under the strain of endless human population growth through our selfish exceptionalism. This is neither nihilism nor existentialism. This is the reality of both a philosophical and ecological crisis.

The first two questions posed here still await an answer. There is no real reason for humans to occupy—for that is what they do, in the most politically arrogant way—the earth. Yet, somehow, some would take my repudiation of my species as defaulting to murder, genocide, or population "control" (shorthand for Western supremacy over developing nations). The concept of anti-natalism kills no one, it targets no groups, and it does not seek to limit certain populations. That human thinking of anti-natalism immediately conjures violence over ethical grace in ceasing to reproduce is more telling of anthropocentrism than of anti-natalism. To deny reproduction as ethical kills no one, no violence is perpetrated, nothing is lost. The world can only open up at the point where it exists for more than one species and more than one kind of human. Whether exceptionalism is individual ("my child will be different") or species-driven (humans are better than all other species), it is as an ideology and an actuality at once violent, ecocidal, and narcissistically delusional.

Even within human exceptionalism, the expectation to reproduce raises the issue of "not all humans" (translation: not all misogynists). Women have historically been and remain designated as incubators for species continuity, while men spread their "blameless" seed everywhere in the same way as their misogyny or patriarchy. This perceived parthenogenesis, where women are blamed for being single parents, or blamed for being child "less" and thus having no purpose, shows that for women, our purpose has not had the luxury of ecumenical or philosophical questions of why we are here. Like the industries that rape and exploit female nonhuman animals to profit from their misery through milk or eggs or pet breeding, human questions of purpose don't include women because our purpose has already been designated. While the Sphinx's riddle to Oedipus allotted man his own three ages—the child, the adult, the aged sage—women are relegated to theirs via breeding: the child (but sexy because verging on controllable potential), the fecund woman, the witch or crone. It is easy to say that women now have the choice. Experience as a woman and an anti-natalist shows the choice is there, but so too are the outrages and death threats and general default position of "why not?"

Ecosophically, there are larger issues than personal choice at stake. What of Earth and its other inhabitants if we continue to breed? What happens when we rethink this or, better still, remove reproduction from the narrative? Are childfree women, tormented and tortured as witches no matter what their age (as both Brunschweiger and I have experienced personally due to our work), still women, reminiscent of Monique Wittig's claim that lesbians are not women? Taken out of the enforced hetero-reproductive matrix, childfree women can be women on their own terms. The burgeoning field of "care" ecology and philosophy shows that perhaps a more maternalistic relation with the earth, activism, and ethics is something all humans need to adopt in order to redeem ourselves from the destruction we cause. We can retain the maternal theory feminism has given us beyond the imago-filling production of mini-me children that fosters equally violent dividing lines of family, lineage, clan, nation, all of course in and with the name of the father as the orienting signifier. Anti-natalism queers care, ecology, feminism, and ethics while harming nothing. Can breeding claim the same?

For the environment, for feminism, for marginalized lives on this precarious Earth, this book raises important contemplations that are integral to dismantling anthropocentric dominion and human exceptionalism.

Patricia MacCormack is an Australian scholar and a professor of Continental Philosophy at Anglia Ruskin University of Cambridge, UK. She has published extensively in the areas of animal studies, feminism, queer theory, and posthuman ethics. Patricia's monographs *Cinesexuality* and *Posthuman Ethics* and *The Animal Catalyst* collection have been key readings on curricula internationally. Her latest book, *The Ahuman Manifesto*, was released in 2020. She currently works on an impact case study on inclusivity in mental health and criminal justice, especially in relation to issues of sexual difference and transgender rights.

1
ONE WOMAN'S *VIA CRUCIS*

Is it okay to still have children, US Representative Alexandria Ocasio-Cortez wondered in 2019. She's definitely not the only one to ask this question. The English singer Blythe Pepino is one of those to put her decision into action by founding BirthStrike, which is now called Grieving Parenthood in the Climate Crisis. This phenomenon is not really new: it occurred time and again all over the world, especially in the 1970s, the golden years of feminism in Europe. The most important reasons not to have kids are the state of our environment and feminist aspects, so the first two chapters deal with these two issues.

This book will explore what childfree means and why couples and women without children are not childless—but childfree. Amy Blackstone writes that childfree women are seen as "dangerous oddities" (Blackstone, 2014). Somehow it just seems unnatural for females. Maybe because it means that you're doing something really empowering instead of doing what all the other women seem to do—fulfilling a social norm.

Why is the difference between *childfree* and *childless* so important? Well, the suffix *–less* obviously contains negative connotations. *Jobless, heartless*: it's better to have a job and a heart and we are meant to believe that it's also better to have a child—or even better, child*ren*. Furthermore, many parents—who consider themselves superior human beings because they successfully

5

managed to procreate—use this term in a derogatory way to talk about us fine childfree folk. Apart from these two important aspects there is another one. There are in fact real childless people: those who desperately want to be parents but somehow don't have fully functioning reproductive organs, not the right partner, etc.

This book isn't about the latter category. They usually turn their sex life into a nightmare trying and trying. This book is about people who voluntarily decide not to have kids, who embrace this lifestyle wholeheartedly. It's them we're going to have a closer look at.

This debate is much more difficult in Germany compared to the U.S. or Great Britain, despite their nasty nationalistic turns in recent years, given Brexit and the election of the sexist, racist, vulgar agitator, and follower of antisemitic conspiracy myths, Donald J. Trump. Trumpism and the new Right in Europe and their reactionary family-focused ideology are among the topics in Chapter 3, where political reasons to remain childfree are analyzed.

Take *West Side Story*'s song "America" from 1957. The starting point is the heat in Puerto Rico and the fact that, as Anita sings, "the population" is "always growing." Female self-determination? No way. Manhattan is the new world and the dream of the female protagonists of *West Side Story*. We may well turn that pursuit of individual happiness—without ignoring the dialectics of capitalism, cultural industry—into a feminist attack on today's new Right in the U.S. and Europe.

We all know that capitalism is the core contributor of CO_2, including state capitalism like in China and their one-party dictatorial system. I will not blame women for being the core persons responsible for climate change, of course. That kind of blame might absolve capitalism of its huge impact in nature's destruction and our existing socio-economic systems that see human beings as nothing but a means to an end.

But women who give birth are expected to present themselves as heroines who might make the world better. Perhaps the opposite is true. I want to embolden those who deliberately do not want to reproduce, for philosophical, feminist, anti-patriarchal, or other political or social reasons.

This book wants to encourage both young and not so young people to be proud non-parents, free and independent people, or even intellectuals. Following Friedrich Nietzsche, I want to plea for a re-evaluation of all values. What if the breeders are to blame for the current ecological, social, and cultural crises of the West—and not those who refuse to reproduce for a huge number of reasons?

Take a lovely morning, afternoon, or even night and the intimate situation of two people who are in true love in the first place. At some point, he argues, "Darling, you have wonderful eyes, wouldn't it be a shame to not produce a mini-version of yours?" For mainstream people and followers of the pro-natalist paradigm or patriarchal ideology, that might be a trigger for a lovely night. For those independent thinkers, though, that very statement might end every single sense of eroticism in this situation. Why does someone need a mini version of these eyes? Does that not include the degradation of these wonderful, colorful, shining, ecstatic eyes of the beloved partner?

Do childfree people have better sex? This book will try to give you some fascinating answers to this question. My sociological approach follows Bruno Latour (Latour 2005), who wants us to describe and observe minute phenomena, not to filter or discipline.

Chapter 4 outlines philosophical aspects concerning reproduction, first and foremost anti-natalism as a way to prevent suffering. If you introduce a rather traditional pro-natalist country like Germany to these obviously "new" concepts (at least for the mainstream) around the childfree lifestyle, you are sure to suffer as well, as the following story shows.

1.1 Germany, 2019

When I came back to school after spring break, the atmosphere in my staff room was frosty—to put it mildly. I was met by hostile glares from usually friendly (or at least polite) colleagues. My boss wanted me in her office, ASAP. What had happened?

I had published a book. That isn't a crime, is it? Well, it turned out to be one in this case. . . . The book in question, *Childfree Not Childless: A Manifesto*, appeared on March 6, 2019. My Bavarian hometown Regensburg was enjoying one week's spring break when the local newspaper featured an article about the teacher who doesn't want to have babies for environmental reasons—me.

National uproar ensued. Why all this hatred directed toward a woman who wants to save the earth by not giving birth? My cute little grammar school in the picturesque medieval town somehow wasn't able to grasp this strange concept. So, I sat through several long meetings, while supporters started to compare me to Galileo Galilei. Personally, I felt more like a witch about to be burned. And that's a pretty weird feeling! The Spanish Inquisition is way in the past, you might think. But suddenly, it rears its ugly head again.

In essence, I wrote about being childfree because of the pitiful condition of today's world. About being childfree as an act of defying patriarchy. About being childfree from a philosopher's point of view: the anti-natalist perspective.

Being child*free* (or just referring to yourself as such) enrages German people—and not only them—to an unexpected extent. Why is that? Do they really still think that the world shall be healed by the German spirit? This horrifying notion came more and more true when they started making comments. "Go to Africa and tell *them* to stop breeding" featured prominently. When I pointed out that one German child roughly used as many resources as *thirty*

African kids, they didn't say a word. But their eyes kept shooting daggers at me. They hated me even more for providing them with information they really didn't want to hear.

BirthStrike is a concept well-known and widely accepted throughout the English-speaking world, but good old Germany was absolutely shocked by the first official announcement that having babies might be a poor choice if you *really* aim for an environmentally friendly lifestyle.

Tons of articles about climate change appeared daily in our papers, full of helpful advice on how to make your own big contributions: AVOID LONG-DISTANCE FLIGHTS, EAT LESS MEAT, LEAVE YOUR CAR IN THE GARAGE FROM TIME TO TIME. . . . BUT NEVER, EVER HAVE ONE CHILD LESS!

Remember the three Rs: REDUCE, REUSE, RECYCLE and conveniently "forget" the fourth and most important one: DON'T *REPRODUCE*! The UN's seventeen Sustainable Development Goals (SDGs) also miss the most important one.

This taboo, a typically German blind spot, was broken by yours truly and soon the first stone was cast: Germany's *Bild-Zeitung* bestowed the title of *heartless teacher* upon me, and many others followed suit. One supporter wrote that the adjective applied to me would probably never have been chosen if I had been a man. (She might be right there!)

But *why* on Earth did they not understand that I was trying to save the world *for* my students, first and foremost? I wanted them to have a future that deserved the name, not some horrible dystopia characterized by water wars and social unrest. My colleagues proceeded. One of them wrote on a sheet of paper: I'M A PROUD MOTHER OF THREE, I'M NOT SELFISH, I'M NOT BRAINWASHED. Then she glued it on her locker. Obviously some kind of role model, three or four other offended mothers copied her sheet and also glued it to their lockers. One should know that between 1880 and 1957—with exemptions—female teachers in Germany had to be celibate.

Their next move was to stick an article about my "scandalous thesis," written by a local journalist, on the staff room's notice board, collecting signatures below. Needless to say, the journalist didn't agree with my point of view.

I'm a fighter, so I could cope with all that pretty well. What did get to me, though, was the announcement that I would be removed from my ethics classes the following semester. I still can't believe how anything so outrageous and dictatorial could be done to an environmentalist and a feminist who was only trying to make the world a better place!

When I asked about the motivation for such an extraordinary move, I was given a surprisingly plain answer: there were some concerned parents who didn't want their kids to be manipulated—by me. So, let me get this straight: If you try to save the planet, you're a manipulative cow not fit to teach children ethics?! I can't get over this.

If you are a feminist, you're used to being ridiculed. Insults by men and women are quite normal. If you are a radical feminist, you'll probably have received at least one death threat. Anita Sarkeesian, for example, who founded the website Feminist Frequency, criticized sexism in video games—which led to death threats for years. Feminist author Rebecca Solnit agrees: Progressive feminist voices are often under severe attack, with the goal to eliminate them completely. If you resist, this is great and courageous, but it takes its toll. Solnit also writes that combatting the attacks depletes our energies, which we could employ differently. Some of us allow the bullies to win, being threatened by the violence they display. It's tiresome and one tends to develop certain fears if you have to face hate-stalkers all the time.

Women in general are frequent victims of hate speech. There are typical strategies to defame them: devaluing everything they do and say, debasing their physical appearance, and depreciating their personalities. There are differences in the language used by the misogynists. Some of them are intelligent beings, many of them are not; but anti-feminism is a common phenomenon in times of global backlash and is not at all restricted to the working class.

If you are a childfree radical feminist, you're the most horrible abomination for all masculinists on Earth because you challenge patriarchy most fundamentally. So, it's no surprise when some of them decide to turn to criminal actions, like sending hate mail.

One envelope waiting for me in my pigeonhole was addressed to the *murderess Verena Brunschweiger*, written in red ink. I didn't open it. I threw it into the next bin at hand instead. Others might have read it; but why should I? I know what to expect from letters like that one. And afterward? Pressing charges against some unknown, anonymous criminal? There are many different and more useful ways to employ my time and energy.

Usually, you receive your death threats online, of course, as it's easier and less expensive. The guy sending me his letter had to purchase a stamp.

Due to a significant increase in brutalization in general, criminals quite frequently document their activities online. If you think of the antisemitic killing spree in Halle, Germany, on October 9, 2019, for example, you'll notice that the murderer technically enabled others to be direct witnesses to his abominable crime via gamification. This is relevant in this context because men like him always name feminism as one of the major problems of today's world. He supposes it's the feminists' fault if modern women have fewer children; he also claims that Jews are vile people only fit to be extinguished, along with other minorities his aggressions are directed to: refugees/foreigners, homosexuals, leftists, etc. I'll come back to this important interdependence.

I recently got an email asking how my "killing humankind" was progressing. The second sentence was regret about my decision "against life, pro death," culminating in the third and last sentence that he would have loved to have children with me. Well, thank you! I normally don't care too much about what people make of me, but in this case, I was shaking with rage.

Obviously, he hated my opinion. Yet he fantasized about multiple nonprotected rapes. Brilliant! Threatening to rape feminists is as old as feminism itself. Whenever women rebel against societal norms, several men are ready to defend patriarchy, using every possible weapon. Rape is a classic. . . .

Luckily, I work part-time at school—in order to have more time for my passion: singing. Regensburg's beautiful city center is not only a UNESCO-World Heritage site, it also contains lots of museums, art galleries, book shops, and a very fine theater. The opera department of this theater allows excellent amateurs to join the professionals from time to time, e.g., when Verdi's Nabucco is staged. Then the conductor invites people like me to perform alongside the professional singers who are in the opera choir. We're called the *extra choir*.

So, when I entered "my" theater after said book publishing fiasco, I was not sure what to expect. But—surprise! One neutral sentence here, one "congrats!" there. . . . And that was it. I couldn't believe it. Obviously, there are workplaces where it's okay to be childfree and others where it's not. Easy as that. Some of you might think that this special situation is due to a lack of mothers and fathers working at a theater. Not true. My best friend, a professional singer at Theater Regensburg, has two children—and he doesn't mind my decision and activism at all. On the contrary, he exclaimed enthusiastically: "Oh, Verena, how cool! Then my kids will have less competition in the water wars!" He's one smart dad. But at the theater, he's not alone. Almost every man who works there has two kids—and not one of them criticized me. Far from it: they expressed their admiration for my courage and were, in fact, quite happy because of the success of my book.

Jokes were made. When I was roaming the corridors backstage, someone would shout: "Here comes the first really famous person working at Theater Regensburg!" Another colleague would add: "Ah, our TV star!" This was completely different from what I was going through at school. Maybe it's just because artists are brilliant people. They definitely are, but is this the only reason?

A significant aspect is that there are people from more than two hundred countries working peacefully side by side at this theater. Broad-mindedness is therefore a sine qua non. But if you take into account that there are many Koreans in the choir and orchestra, and that family is traditionally very important in Korea, it's rather a surprise that not one single Korean mother or father reacted negatively when they were confronted with my book. Far from it. Two of the dads supported this idea. They immediately understood that anti-natalism isn't about the children (or adults) already existing. It's never one's own fault that you're here, but it's your "fault" if you reproduce. Nevertheless, the Asian people didn't feel criticized at all; one of them kept sending his kids to my house—*of course.*

On the other hand, some *German* parents didn't want me to teach their children anymore. And there's the rub. It's the *German* mindset that is so easily offended, that values German children above everything else. . . . And we're directly back in the 1930s!

The German mentality in general—if there is such a thing—is unfortunately still quite conducive to putting yourself and your family first.

One example underlining these unpleasant tendencies is this one: in Ukraine, sick children don't go to school. They are allowed to stay at home until they have fully recovered. Not so in Germany. That's also why our schools have flu epidemics throughout fall, winter, and spring. Students with hacking coughs are sent to school without thought—they might miss something—infecting all the other people in the classroom (including the teachers). Only the coronavirus has brought about some changes there. Other people are never as important as your own goals and interests—a lesson the pupils learn quite soon from their parents in this country.

Another example is also from school, but highly significant: it's extremely "uncool" to study. Learning your vocabulary, doing your homework—this is for noobs. This trend is particularly prominent among male teenagers in Germany, who are so cool because they have worse grades than their female peers (somehow, they still manage to earn more later on, but that's a different topic). They think they are brilliant enough to sail through school, getting top grades for doing nothing. This hubristic attitude is typical of German people in general. So of course, their children are always better and more important than those of other nations or people—although most parents would never admit that because being politically correct is something you just do; your real thoughts and feelings are for close friends and family.

If you ask a student from South Korea about his vacation plans, he'll reply without any sign of embarrassment that he'll be studying. A German male his age would never avow that. Education, politeness, and improving oneself are great values among South Koreans. It's no surprise that their birth rate is one of the lowest in the world! In general, they aren't ruthless at all and take pride in making the most of themselves instead of breeding brainlessly.

Another mother working at Theater Regensburg told me that she had come to Germany from Azerbaijan with great hopes and expectations. She had been informed that Germany was a country where everything seemed to be fair and just, clean and clear. . . . Then she moved to Regensburg and was more than a little surprised. German bureaucracy did this artist's head in, and she was shocked when she found out that corruption exists in this country too. Then she followed the reports about my case and couldn't believe how pro-natalist the German press was! Said the mother of two. More importantly, she said she had come here to enjoy the famous German freedom of opinion. She was absolutely shocked by the reactions from many people at school and at the ministry of education. *What about your freedom of speech*, she almost yelled at me over coffee. I sat there helplessly, shrugging. I couldn't help her either.

Pro-natalism can be described as the promotion of baby-making for a nation's social, political, and especially economic purposes. It also teaches girls and women that kids are synonymous with stability and the answer to the big question of life's meaning. Motherhood is portrayed as some kind of higher calling, not only a choice. Stepping outside this path isn't or shouldn't be conceivable. Pro-natalism masks itself as the unmarked, the norm. It's rarely questioned; it's just the way the world works, it needs no justification. At least that's the mainstream opinion. I want to challenge this notion.

In 2019, Leslie Kern published her book *Feminist City*. Despite its title, the first chapter is nevertheless about mothers. Only later on do we read about friends, lesbians, etc. But the most important aspect seems to be motherhood. In a "feminist" book, by a self-proclaimed feminist author! She could have called her work *City of Women* or something along these lines, but why on earth *Feminist*

City? She does quote Virginia Woolf, who was childfree and a real feminist, but she doesn't appear to fully understand her message.

Gustave Flaubert's *flâneur* is notorious. The French writer used this term to describe a certain type of gentleman, walking the streets of Paris aimlessly, with elegance and an open mind, composing poems in his head. To put it simply, we could say the *flâneur* is similar to Oscar Wilde's dandy and prefers to be inspired by leisurely walks in the streets. He's completely free and can follow anyone and anything on a whim. Kern takes this figure and writes about the female version of it—the *flâneuse*. Great idea. But she spoils everything by asking why there isn't any *flâneuse* pushing a stroller. . . . That's exactly the point! If a woman has a baby, she isn't really free anymore and cannot live the life of a free woman, roaming the streets, deciding on impulse whether to stay out the whole night. The aspect of why so many childfree women are also feminists will be dealt with in Chapter 2.

Kern complains that she got so much advice on what to eat, wear, and do when she was pregnant. Sadly, she doesn't acknowledge the omnipresent pressure that made her, like many other women, succumb to this mandatory act. She does admit, though, that the biological needs of a newborn make it virtually impossible to enjoy your life without interruption. So why did she become pregnant, one can't help wondering, if she misses the life of the *flâneuse* so much?

Another blind spot of Kern's is that she wants people to show more consideration for mothers. Fine. In the next episode she tells her readers that she herself often behaved inconsiderately as a mom, for example not paying attention with her stroller, which caused a friendly helper to topple down the subway steps.

It's no wonder Kern doesn't grasp radical feminism's attitude toward the sexist patriarchal capitalist system of the exploitation of women and their bodies and prostitution, either. Kern defends pimps and johns by buying into the myth of the happy sex worker.

Consequently, she sides with science fiction author Samuel R. Delany, who in *Times Square Red, Times Square Blue* (1999) misses porn theaters and prostitution around New York City's iconic location. The 1990s cleanup campaigns and zero tolerance policy under Mayor Rudy Giuliani led to a very different Times Square, à la Disneyland, as Delany and Kern put it.

Interestingly, feminist geographer and director Brett Story (2013) also talks about this phenomenon and contrasts the "old" face of Times Square with the new one, which is considered "family-friendly." But this is it! This is what's getting on my nerves all the time, this ancient whore/saint dichotomy. As a woman, you have to choose: slut or mother. There don't seem to be many other options. If you're not in favor of prostitution, you have to be a person who celebrates family values. What about the radical childfree feminists like me who find both systems detrimental to women? Both are patriarchal institutions dominating women's bodies, modifying and using them according to their own needs and wishes. We have to fight both, if we really want to free women.

Rebecca Solnit, on the other hand, states clearly that attacks on women's physical integrity are seldom friendly offers by attractive people. There are so many misconceptions about prostitution that US psychologist, author, and activist Melissa Farley, who wrote several books about prostitution and human trafficking, also published a paper about myths and facts related to the sex industry (2009). Men who buy female bodies are not nice guys; they don't respect women as personalities. It's always about power.

Brett Story mentions more control, too. Not only are there now cameras everywhere, which do offer a feeling of security for some, but private apps for social networks like Nextdoor provide their users with ample opportunities to denounce their fellow human beings if they don't correspond to certain criteria. Single, homeless, older women, for instance, have an incredibly hard life in our patriarchal society, which favors young families. People with disabilities are never as worthy of support as people with small kids. Western states (and not only those) are incredibly pro-natalist and we have to acknowledge and possibly change this.

Obviously, intersectionality is always important (in the way professor Kimberlé Crenshaw understands it: race, class, and gender, as well as (dis)abilities etc. often intersect/overlap), as my example of the senior single woman without a home demonstrates.

The motherhood mandate is stronger than ever before. It pervades our whole life. In the workplace, it is what drives people to bring babies to the office, what makes them ask inappropriate questions ("When are you going to have kids?" etc.), what lets parents leave early because they somehow think their kids' school play is more important than your Italian lesson—and the vast majority encourages this. It's also what makes so many moms create blogs, often selling child products online (clothes, toys, food, you name it), which are a big hit (the annual turnover is astronomic). It's what explains child tax benefits. This list is infinite.

In the U.K., several studies confirm that those who don't have kids are expected to pick up extra work, work longer, take holiday time nobody else wants, and face unpleasant questions and comments concerning their no-kids status.

Indeed, breeder privilege seems to be a big problem in several countries and it's high time to listen to the childfree and childless instead of shoveling more and more benefits on whining parents! Solnit agrees: There are those who succumb and accept this role everyone seems to push you into, and there are the rebels. Of course, the latter path is much stonier; but it's absolutely worth it.

It all starts with this initiation rite every woman goes through: the catcalling, the attention of boys/men you don't really want, being ogled on the bus, suddenly feeling uncomfortable in shorts, etc. Finally, the message is always this one: you vulnerable woman, choose me, I'll "protect" and impregnate you, and isn't that what you want, being a woman?

It's almost impossible to escape this never-ending story. One student told me online that home-schooling was better because it reduced bullying, which made others laugh instantly—what about cyberbullying?! You're not okay the way you are—so be happy that "cool" guys consider you worthy enough. Solnit adds that it's easy to target young women/girls, because self-doubts are instilled from a very early age. Others know better: your parents, your siblings, your classmates, your teachers, your favorite stars. So, if they all say, motherhood is tremendously important for every woman, aren't they right? Isn't this what you should do, even if you're not one hundred percent sure about it yourself?

Solnit repeats several times that women are always trained to please men, to look their best, and so on. She encourages girls to reject the misogynistic standards boys and men apply when they assume to judge their appearance. This seems like old news, yet there are myriads of girls and women suffering because of lookism, ageism, slut-shaming, and fat-shaming, but also body-shaming in general. (Rebecca Solnit was told she was "too thin" and had to endure "jokes" about starving children.) The list is endless. Solnit used her imagination to dream of places where women were more than trophies, decoration, or broodmares. This is also my vision of a beautiful world.

The outside world, however, seemed to side with the majority of colleagues at my school.

At least, booksellers did. Usually, if there's a local author (we have quite a handful), the biggest chain bookstore here sticks huge posters with their picture everywhere, advertising the publication.

Normally, there are also readings. Not in my case. No portrait, no reading, nothing. Not even the book itself was on display. Windows of other booksellers were checked out—same situation.

A fan living in Austria wrote to me, also telling me about this highly unusual phenomenon. Customers who insisted on asking for the book were often told blatant lies, such as that it wasn't available or the store had run out of copies. A primary boycott! Nazi book burnings come to mind because obviously some breeders are so enraged by my book they just can't take it being on display because it's *degenerate art.*

It's quite incredible that a completely harmless book listing various good reasons for a childfree life should be considered so evil—in the year 2019! In 2020, the *Childfree Rebellion*, my second book on this topic, suffered a similar fate.

But of course, right-wing parties have always placed special emphasis on values like family and tradition. Increasing their respective national populations via birth rate is their pet project. In Germany, the AfD (Alternative for Germany) repeatedly stresses the importance of German children. In Hungary, Hungarian kids are considered top notch. In Italy, Italian children; in France, it's French babies they need—ad infinitum. Pro-natalist governments—and there are no anti-natalist governments—reward people who opt for reproduction, although it's crystal clear that Earth's capacity to bear humans has been exceeded for a while. They do this because most voters are parents, and the politicians don't want to lose even one of them.

In 2010, the German politician Thilo Sarrazin published his book *Deutschland schafft sich ab* ("Germany Is Digging Its Own Grave," as *The Guardian* translated it. Or: "Germany Is Doing Away with Itself," as others suggested). Sarrazin's main idea is that German people don't breed enough, but Muslims living here do, so therefore, they will take over the whole country eventually. What a nightmare! This racist, fascist thesis seems to have struck a chord with the majority of the German population, at least secretly. There were some half-hearted attempts to criticize him and that was about it. Needless to say, his book was prominently displayed, with huge piles at the entrance of every bookstore! There is still a lot of the old Nazi in "modern" Germans.

It was in 1873 when Otto von Bismarck's laws outlined the correct behavior for his officials: the main duty was obedience. Officials were people who had to obey the emperor's every order— *even if it turned out to be a questionable one.* There were plenty of different sanctions for those who didn't fulfill their duty. Authority-abiding people were indispensable for Bismarck, and for modern German institutions this is still the case.

In 1933, there was a new law to modify the civil service system to the Third Reich's needs. It was now possible not only to remove Jews from this apparatus, but all other dissidents as well. Well, that's history, isn't it? Everything has changed, right? No, it hasn't. Not at all. German laws for civil servants are still more or less *the same.* True, it's not an emperor but a senior official we have to obey nowadays.

After the war, there were several re-education programs. Yet the laws for state officials didn't really change. You have to obey, even if your boss gives you an unconstitutional order, unless you'd commit a punishable crime. And if you have such a boss? Can you tell your story? No, of course not; that would interfere with your duty to keep confidential!

There are certain unalienable rights, one might assume. Not for German civil servants. Even if our constitution guarantees freedom of speech, our reality unfortunately looks quite different.

In Germany, the AfD gains more and more popularity and if they use this relic, this stupid excuse for a law regulating state officials' duties, history can easily repeat itself.

If you want a job as a teacher in Bavaria, for instance, you're not allowed to be a member of the *Linkspartei* (Germany's left-wing party) because our ruling parties consider it extremist (which is not true). It's clear why they do this: If you reject dissenters from the start, you'll have fewer problems later on, even if you are subject to directives anyway. The purpose of all those laws combined is to have an apparatus of civil servants who will never, ever disobey.

So why this excursion into German history—specifically, its system of civil service? Because our contemporary population expects a certain moderate behavior if they find out that you belong to this caste. They wouldn't expect you to write books *against* something, especially not against traditional German Holy Grails, like prostitution (Germany is sadly known as Europe's biggest brothel) or prospective future *German* generations.

Another important aspect in this case is that my boss can arbitrarily dismiss me from my ethics classes and there is nothing I can do. I could file a formal complaint, but that wouldn't get me anywhere. There is absolutely no legitimate reason not to give me ethics courses next semester, but my boss can do it because she has the power to do so.

Three months after the publication of the book I was "invited" to Munich, Bavaria's capital, where I had the honor of meeting three representatives of the ministry of education—my employer. My local school boss came along, too, and sided with the three people who disappointed more than any other individuals. I had expected support and encouragement but all I got were words of reproach and threat. From people who have a fiduciary duty! Usually, the employee is defended against vicious attacks, but not in this case. It was more than palpable that I was meant to be fed to the dogs.

This incident did it: I formally requested a leave of absence for a year, which was of course immediately granted. Problem removed.

This didn't go down well with everyone at school. There were indeed colleagues, even among those who had bullied me before, that were quite surprised and dared to ask: *And who's teaching her classes now?* Well, that wasn't my problem anymore, was it? I'll never know which classes they would have assigned to me. One father, who had supported me all along, wrote an outraged letter on my behalf.

This decision was discussed in the local papers, of course. *They* invited me to their "Gala 2019: The Year in Review—Persons Who Struck a Chord."

It's common practice to take a hard line with those few who don't agree with everything the ministry and its representatives utter. If you are not a traditional, conservative kind of person who dislikes any changes, you're already suspicious, untrustworthy. Hence the popular accusation: *Are you really defending our wonderful free democratic basic order?* It's up to you to convince them. If you fail, they can do almost anything to you.

There are several cases in Bavaria that clearly show what type of people the officials want. On December 9, 2019, German journalist Anna Klühspies wrote about Lion, a teacher trainee from Munich who got into trouble because of a rap song he'd produced thirteen years earlier. Like me, Lion was "invited" by the ministry to "talk" about his activities. These talks feel like a telling-off, an impression which Lion, now thirty-five, confirms. The representatives of the ministry of education preach about being a role model, about certain values a public official should stand for. If you criticize the state, you're obviously not one of the eligible candidates. If you're not a fan of Bavaria's new homeland ministry, you're some strange person and it seems to be questionable if you're fit to teach kids. . . . You're an enemy of our constitution if you want to perform a critical song or write a book attacking mainstream "values." Lion teaches at a private school now.

The important question is: How are we supposed to teach teenagers to use their freedom of speech when we aren't allowed to do that ourselves? What kind of message does this send to kids when they have to witness how harshly teachers are disciplined when they go against the grain? This is a scandal many people don't know about and it's vital to inform everyone about the possibilities for right-wing parties in a climate like that. They benefit in these cases; nobody else does. It's about power and obedience, nothing else.

This thesis is supported by the fact that there is a headmaster in Franconia, a region of Germany, who is not only a member of the AfD, but a functionary. Somehow, this didn't seem to bother the bigwigs at the ministry who appointed him. It's *only* left-wing politics and parties they're concerned about. Maybe they just don't realize that fascist tendencies are fostered and facilitated in this way; maybe they just don't know that leftists fight for justice and real equality and don't want to abolish the state.

Yet it seems necessary to warn everyone who considers themselves progressive. Asking and probing about a possible employee's attitudes and dispositions is fine (well, some people don't agree, which is totally understandable), but if one spectrum is not acceptable whereas the more dangerous one is, one can't help but feel a bit uneasy. . . .

That said, patriotism is thinly veiled, anyway. It's even part of the oath one has to swear when you become a public official in Bavaria. Love of our Bavarian home is something we are supposed to teach the pupils. No joke. This fits perfectly if you look at one of the musical productions of Theater Regensburg: *Ludwig II*, the legendary Bavarian king who promoted Richard Wagner and built his fairy-tale castles. Originally, the musical was created for the Neuschwanstein castle that Ludwig built for Wagner, where millions of visitors watched it. When I read the reviews after the musical's first night at Theater Regensburg, I waited for some criticism, but found it lacking in every text that could be found. Given that the young king sings about his dream to become a German *Führer*, this is more than astonishing.

All this is based on history, so it's obviously not necessary to criticize any hint of nationalistic or patriotic ethos. It's also sadly not surprising, especially when a new museum was built in Bavaria: Der Haus der Bayerischen Geschichte (the House of Bavarian History)—an extremely ugly modern building (which cost an enormous sum) near the Danube. The exhibits are mostly objects that show how utterly wonderful Bavaria and its history are. There are no critical words about aspects which are not that great.

Speaking of the papers, on October 16, 2019, the *Straubinger Tagblatt*, a local Bavarian newspaper, published a long interview with me—and somehow the tone had slightly changed. It was obvious that the very young male journalist (twenty-six) was less biased than his older colleagues who usually write about me. He asked quite nicely how I felt half a year after the book's release and also chose an interesting title for his article: ""Herzlos" oder Weltretterin?" ("'Heartless' or Savior of the World?"). He quoted the famous adjective the Bild-Zeitung had used to characterize a woman who doesn't want to procreate. But he added the opposite possibility too. And this was fairly new. Of course, it's also a bit black and white, but *Straubinger Tagblatt* isn't a non-profit organization, it's a newspaper.

The piece also stands out as the overall tone of the debate was still hostile, and the heartless teacher was still considered completely crazy by the German majority, although some Germans had started to hear about BirthStrike and several stars advocating small families for the planet's sake. Fridays For Future didn't help either. German representatives of this movement also stated they were not really sure; it was certainly a difficult decision whether to have kids or not because of climate change. If they ponder this question, it's usually because of the children and the "future" *they're* extremely likely to face, not because of the planet, the animals, people, and plants that are already here! And it's *their* future we're also concerned about. We can't afford to ignore the severe problems and plight many people living nowadays already endure, yet they babble on and on about future generations. . . .

There are huge numbers of people dying in developing countries, yet they are sad because creating more and more first-world babies isn't considered the best thing you can do anymore by everyone! But no worries, there are enough conservatives (and their offspring) in this world who do anything to discredit the ones who behave responsibly. Heaven forbid others might follow their example!

This is also a reason why homophobia is much more common among right-wing parties: their rhetoric is that they can't have children "naturally" and if they do have kids, they turn them into perverts. It's shocking how many people still think that way. There are even women's groups, for instance in Germany, who proclaim that they fight pedophilia when it's actually homosexuality they have a problem with. For some women, sadly, it seems hard to accept that there are men who don't fancy them or who don't want to sire any children. Their image of men is simplistic and not much more advanced than that of right-wing men who consider procreation as the only reason for women to exist.

Religious leaders join in this chorus—as do their supporters. GOD WANTS YOU TO BREED is a credo many young couples have to face when they talk with their own parents. In 2022! There are people out there who really believe homosexuality can be cured; it's a disease or a punishment God can give or take. This always makes me think of the *Big Gay Musical*, an entertaining movie/musical comedy from 2009, where Adam and Steve (funny . . .) meet at a camp designed to cure homosexuals. The movie is full of pretty good jokes and puns. "Look at your camp T-shirt," Steve is told for example, before they sing the show tune "I'm Gonna Go Straight to Heaven."

Clichés about gays (and some about straight people, too) feature prominently in the musical, but it's always light, amusing, and never offensive, although the issue itself is serious and causes several teenagers each year to commit suicide. That's why institutions like Gay Help Line are so important. Gay and lesbian people sometimes report that their parents are actually fine with their sexuality, the only thing they are sad about is that they won't have "real" grandchildren. Pro-natalism is omnipresent.

Adoption for homosexual couples is still illegal in many countries. Think of Uganda, for example, where homosexuality itself can threaten your very existence (death penalty!). A lesbian I know personally was raped in Sicily in order to "awaken her taste for men." The criminals didn't care that this was the best way to make her detest men for the rest of her life, which she hadn't before. . . .

Also, in Russia and other Eastern European countries, homophobia is still widely tolerated, whereas it's officially extinct in Germany. But laws alone don't change people's mentality overnight and there's still lots of daily homophobia in the streets. In a speech at a Christopher Street Day rally for gay pride in 2019, a young gay man said that he was not comfortable walking around holding hands with his boyfriend. No heterosexual couple has to waste one single thought on that, but there's always a slight fear left in him. Too many stupid comments or even attacks have taught him to be careful, he said, and never relax. Many famous or semi-famous people who are gay tell us about homophobia and discrimination they experienced because of it. Lord Alfred Douglas's love that dare not speak its name might be a thing of the past, but only in the western hemisphere and not in every hamlet there is. Verbal abuse is still quite common. Unfortunately, I witnessed it personally during a demonstration for animal rights in Regensburg, when a young man wearing a skirt was insulted by an older man. Drag queens living in a city as open as Berlin talk about the violence they often have to face—and not only when they are in full drag! Candy Crash, for instance, who has short blond hair and often wears jeans and a shirt, is the victim of discrimination in this outfit too. A hint of make-up, a slight swagger, or an earring sometimes is enough to provoke homophobes.

Accepting homosexuality as such doesn't mean the automatic acceptance of the rights for gay people to adopt. Many couples suffer because of that (and many children, too, who could have a wonderful home). We definitely need laws that aren't as strict in this respect. And while the general situation might be satisfactory in Germany's bigger cities, it's not as good as in Denmark, Iceland, or Canada. Canadian premier Pierre Trudeau showed up at a Christopher Street Day party wearing a tight pink shirt and showing some bare midriff. Can anyone imagine former German chancellor Angela Merkel doing the same? This remark is neither sexist nor ageist: I'm the first one to defend the chancellor's looks, and there have been nasty debates about her hairstyle alone for decades. Not to mention discussions about the cleavage she displayed when she appeared at the Wagner festival in Bayreuth in a purple dress. *This* was discussed; her endorsement of an antisemitic spectacle less so. To gain popularity, she also attended matches of Germany's national soccer team, and went to their locker room to congratulate them. This of course was frequently commented on: Does she have a certain predilection for muscular young men in shorts? Why is she criticized for being childfree? For having married a second time? Former chancellor Gerhard Schröder is on his umpteenth wife, this time a young Asian, and nobody cares.

"And I declared that the dead, who had already died, are happier than the living, who are still alive," says Ecclesiastes 4:2–3 (NIV). "But better than both is the one who has never been born, who has not seen the evil that is done under the sun." This citation offers one of many examples that even religious texts themselves aren't pure pro-natalism, but the interpreters and believers read them that way. This phenomenon often occurs with other topics. It's easy to convince the gullible of certain interpretations, manipulating them in a way that benefits the state or the religious institution in question.

The press and politicians of all shades usually don't celebrate low birth rates either—but they should start doing that if the planet is supposed to exist a bit longer! Almost nobody who wants to be/ remain popular has the courage to do so, because sadly, many parents are rather easily offended. The question has to be asked: Do we all have to be breeder-pleasers? They have so much power, it has to be broken! Or at least not glorified even more. . . . The response of the typical German, lashing out at people who have a different opinion while celebrating their open-mindedness, has to be called what it is: criminal behavior revealing a mask of pure hypocrisy.

In Finland, authorities even hid science magazines featuring an article about this very topic: fewer children being a benefit, not a curse. We need low and lower birth rates if we want to survive. But somehow, conservatives (and some others) just don't want to grasp the simple concept that endless exponential growth (economically or of our own numbers) is not possible on a finite planet! Nevertheless, you read the usual nonsense everywhere about some kind of invented "need" for ever more growth, rather than the absolutely necessary celebration of reduced human impact.

From time to time, we come across graffiti or posters that try to point out that ever more people aren't the solution to our problems. They're mainly in big cities, where you can occasionally find really open-minded people thinking outside the box. In Melbourne, Procreation Rebellion sprayed HAVING CHILDREN under several stop signs—a brilliant idea. In the Netherlands or Portugal you can see posters with the caption CELEBRATE LOW BIRTH RATES! This is street art or political activism at its best: it creates awareness, criticizes, but doesn't really offend. The Great Decrease is another interesting organization promoting small families, using slogans LIKE SHRINK TOWARD ABUNDANCE. Sadly, these voices are often unheard or the majority doesn't take them seriously; in both cases, those guys lose, too, although they tried to prevent the worst.

If you reach a certain age (usually, they leave you alone till you've finished your studies) the people around you will start nagging, especially if you're in a heterosexual relationship. This is a universal fact. People from many different countries tell the same story: their own parents, partner's parents, friends, neighbors, colleagues etc. started to interfere with their lives by asking about their reproductive plans. But there's hope: More and more young couples answer that concerns about the environment are their main reason not to procreate. Are they on to something?

2
ECOLOGY

2.1 Overpopulation and Our Environment

Reading about climate change and how to fight it, you'll inevitably come across the standard omnipresent recommendations: fly *less*, eat *less* meat, use your bike once in a while. . . . These contributions are important, no doubt, but are they enough?

Even many right-wingers have been convinced by the fact that there really seems to be some kind of human-made climate change that could possibly harm us. And what gets to them—the us is now also referring to the West, not only to those poor saps in Africa and Asia that lots of them don't care about anyway.

The water wars predicted for 2040 in Europe are already a brutal reality in, for example, India. In the summer of 2019, one woman was stabbed to death by a neighbor fighting over water. Organizations like Population Matters or Population Counts collect and share articles about such events occurring on a daily basis. This detail alone shows how much is going on, how many incidents take place already all over the world, and they don't become less true only because some stubborn Westerners prefer running around with their eyes wide shut.

As a result of its data collection, Population Counts asks if now is a good time to be adding 240,000 new people to the planet every day. (Others estimate the figure to be 400,000 per day.) This is the core of the whole discussion: Not only do you have to ask yourself what you're doing to the environment if you add a new human being, you also have to ponder what you're inflicting on this innocent new person by bringing them into such a world (cf. Chapter 4). This is by no means a purely philosophical question (it may have been one several hundred years ago), but a question of life and death. If there are wars over scarce resources; if the air is not breathable any longer; if there are more and more diseases and deaths related to climate change—are these really experiences you want your child to have?

Hans Joachim Schellnhuber, a German professor who founded the Potsdam Institute for Climate Impact in 1992, talks about millions of climate refugees in the next decades (Schellnhuber 2015). Africans and Asians who can't live in their country any longer will come to other continents, hoping for better conditions there. Massive heat waves and droughts as well as devastating floods, are already reducing habitable regions in developing countries.

2.2 Animals

And let's not talk about animals. They always fare worse. The habitat of many wonderful creatures, like giraffes, rhinos, and zebras, has been destroyed over decades, intentionally and systematically. Some actions from the World Wildlife Fund, for example, do ameliorate the situation a bit, but this can never be enough to save species we all love. If we continue like this, we'll have some single sad specimens in zoos—and no animals living in the wilderness, because their habitat doesn't exist or can't be inhabited anymore due to extreme heat waves, scarce food and drink, and so on.

In October 2019, Zimbabwe announced the death of fifty-five of their elephants due to severe drought. Many others have died due to poaching. The Australian Koala Foundation estimates that there aren't many koalas left in the wild. Its population decline is due to habitat destruction, attacks by domestic dogs, bushfires, and road accidents—all four reasons directly related to humans and their exponentially growing population.

It's not only the land, but the sea suffers too. Run-off from intensive agriculture and industry destroys freshwater and marine environments, killing lots of fish. People also eat too much fish. The amount of tuna taken from the seas has increased by a thousand percent in the last sixty years. The demand has to be curbed. An easy way would be to stay below replacement level concerning reproduction, but unfortunately, this isn't enough anymore. So, we have to make sacrifices concerning our food choices too.

If you eat meat, a creature had to suffer and die for your meal. If you drink milk, an artificially inseminated cow and her calf suffer so you have "your" milk. Veganism is the best choice regarding diet and there's no excuse: hundreds of books show you how to cook absolutely delicious food that doesn't cost much and--much more importantly—doesn't require any animal to suffer. I'd highly recommend the works of Carol J. Adams in this respect; for example, her classic from 1990, *The Sexual Politics of Meat*.

The French philosopher and animal rights activist Corine Pelluchon also wrote several books about animal equality, directly attacking the speciesism of so many humans who still think they are superior. She refers to the great philosopher Arthur Schopenhauer (co-founder of Munich's first animal protection institution) and his ethics of compassion. The way we treat animals shows what kind of people we are. Indeed, our relationship with/attitude toward animals is a kind of mirror telling us who we are or who we've become over centuries. Nonetheless, there remains so much unhappiness, such an amount of injustice, although there are lots of institutions and individuals dedicating their lives to the cause.

As Pelluchon confirms, more than forty-five years after the start of the most recent intellectual efforts to consider the interests of nonhuman animals (such as with the publication of Peter Singer's *Animal Liberation* in 1975), those concerned still suffer. There are many books and arguments and theories, but the main difficulty is putting the ideas into practice to liberate real animals. What are philosophical discussions for? Several aspects can be dealt with in a merely theoretical approach, but seldom has it been as important as in the case of our nonhuman friends.

One thinks of Colin Dann's novel *The Animals of Farthing Wood*, when Toad talks about edible friends and the famous Farthing Wood Oath, which states that while traveling, no animal is going to eat one of the other animals, even if they "usually/naturally" would. What about such an oath for people? We are responsible for our friends, the animals, so why do we eat them?

Wild and domestic animals alike suffer from human inconsideration. Yes, of course, there's this difference everyone knows about: we pamper our cats and dogs and buy irrationally expensive paraphernalia for them, while we eat meat, wear leather shoes, and so on. Pets are just different, we think. We condemn Asians who still eat dog meat, yet having pork-based sausages every day is completely acceptable for many Europeans or Americans.

We have grown accustomed to the institutionalized suffering of farmed animals. In order to be able to stand this, the majority of us ignore the conditions those animals live in—as long as we don't see the pigs we're eating living in pain, squeezed into the tiniest cages. How can we pretend that mammals don't have feelings and dreams, that they suffer like we do? Their last moments on Earth are spent in agony—why is this okay for so many people?

Capitalism is one of the main reasons why people continue to exploit animals for food, fur, and other goods. An especially insightful fact can be found in Lisa Kemmerer's edited volume *Sister*

Species: Women, Animals and Social Justice. Kemmerer points out that there's sexism concerning the world of the animals, too, as it's female mammals who are exploited for their milk and used as incubators.

Another gendered aspect comes to mind: there are more female vegetarians or vegans than male, and it's mostly teenage boys who torture animals. This isn't a surprise, since it's also mostly men who buy sex. Where's the connection? you might ask. Well, if you don't respect other creatures' physical integrity, it's easy to eat meat and to use somebody's vagina/anus as if it really was just a body part to rent. Of course, there are lots of great men doing neither, but there are still too many doing both. . . .

An important role is played by schools: Treating other living beings respectfully should be more valued than it is now in the curriculum. Sometimes, you may talk about this issue in an ethics or philosophy class, but veganism is not something that should be promoted, according to the German curriculum. For the politicians and officials who decide what gets taught, it's always crucial to remain "neutral" so that the students can decide without being influenced. This is pure hypocrisy, because students are already greatly influenced by their parents, peers, the media, and many other sources. So, teachers should be allowed to say in front of a classroom full of teenagers, "I'm vegan and I'm proud of it."

There also should be more shops and bars/cafés where you can eat vegan food. In my city of 152,610 inhabitants there were exactly two vegan cafés, until one of them closed. The remaining café has a reduced menu, so if you have food allergies, your choice is quite limited. That has to improve. In Pisa, Italy, Vegan Come Koala Bar, which is mainly attended by students as it's located in the university area, prepares a wide variety of dishes, including takeout. The lovely young owner explained to me, when I asked him why he chose the koala (and not any other cute herbivore), that he just loved koalas and their tenderness. So, if you ever get the chance to go to Pisa, make sure to take a break at this bar.

Role models are also very valuable. The more vegan actors, influencers, musicians, and other artists who go vegan, the better. A vegan teacher might only achieve so much, but if your favorite YouTube star endorses this lifestyle, things may look different. Several types of motivation have to work together to encourage more people to at least try living vegan; anything and anyone that inspires the population to eat less meat is welcome.

Well, maybe not everyone, if you think of the German vegan cook and author of books on veganism, Attila Hildmann. He's based in Berlin and quite famous, because he regularly posts right-wing or antisemitic videos on his homepage. The police also investigated him due to his openly displayed admiration for deniers of the Holocaust.

Luckily, though, such guys are the exception in the peaceful vegan scene. There is hope, especially if you think of personalities like Jacob Koslowsky, the young dancer who became famous in 2020, when the German gay dating show Prince Charming was aired. Jacob was a favorite and remained in the game for a pretty long time, although one of the contestants made fun of the "bio boy." Jacob had contacted me in 2019 due to my environmental activism and I knew he was an ardent vegan on a mission; so I was surprised to see that he didn't talk about it a lot when he was on air. In fact, Jacob *had* talked about veganism, his chosen lifestyle, quite a lot, he told me. But the channel had cut out most of it, as everyone noticed.

Why does this still happen?

It would have been a great opportunity, not only for young gay people, to see an attractive twenty-nine-year-old with a perfect body talking about one of the most important reasons why he looks that good. There are German soccer stars who still promote the consumption of meat, saying that salad-eaters look sad or sick. Nobody censors them! But the editors cut scenes where an inspiring young dancer, who is also into meditation, talks about fantastic ways to nurture yourself so that it's good for the environment and your physical *and* psychic health.

Nietzsche writes in *Thus Spake Zarathustra* that people still are more apish than any apes. The animal/human boundary shouldn't be so harsh. Many famous writers support this view, for example Franz Kafka and Robert Musil with their talking apes (Red Peter) and their laughing horses ("Can a Horse Laugh?").

In 2018, American musician and activist Chris Korda provoked the audience with her *Fleshdance*: "Cow chicken pig human. What's the difference?" Korda, who is part of VHEMT (the Voluntary Human Extinction Movement), definitely has a point. No boundaries, no differences? Her case is similar to that of young French feminist Pauline Harmange, who writes that she hates all men (though she's married to one of them, one of the very few fine ones). Sometimes, it's necessary to exaggerate to get some attention and success later on. . . . And it's still incredibly easy to break a taboo, which is nonetheless surprising because Western civilization considers itself immensely advanced, open, and tolerant. Yet there are people who are allowed to do almost anything, and there are groups, like women, who aren't allowed to utter certain opinions.

Corine Pelluchon, in her *Manifeste Animaliste*, compares the fight for animals to Abraham Lincoln's efforts against slavery. One might add any fights against any kind of discrimination because it's a human predilection to make a weak minority suffer. Abolition can concern slavery, prostitution, and several other forms and institutions of injustice.

If you attack slavery, racism, and sexism, you also have to attack the cruelty many animals still have to face—whether it's far away or just around the corner. There still are bullfights, there still are people wearing real fur, there still are zoos where animals are kept in tiny cages, there still are people hunting for pleasure, there still are so many people eating meat. Yes, there is the plant-based burger company Beyond Meat in the U.S. But lots of countries don't have similar ideas of substituting plants for meat, and many Americans don't like the idea.

Pelluchon isn't optimistic. She writes that she's not sure whether we'll witness the end of the exploitation of all animals in our lifetimes. Sadly, I agree. There are so many people and entire governments who aren't interested *at all* in animal welfare. Poaching, for instance, is a serious problem in many African and Asian countries. As long as people are poor, someone will always be willing to kill an elephant or a rhino in order to get certain "materials" that can be sold for a profit.

Although bullfighting is being criticized and banned more and more, there are still regions in the world that enjoy nothing more than animals fighting each other. It doesn't have to be bulls, it's also (mostly illegal) dog or cock fights. Such animals are bred in order to kill. Hunting is a popular sport in many nations. Racing different kinds of animals are no pleasure for the participants either, only for the spectators. People for the Ethical Treatment of Animals (PETA) and other organizations have been fighting against the fur industry, yet there are still women who wear real fur and are proud of it.

Zoos, Pelluchon thinks, are not all the same. Whereas some animal rights activists don't accept any type of zoo, others know zoos that aren't the most horrible prisons on Earth but a kind of shelter that contributes to the conservation of threatened species. That said, it's never okay to watch any creatures behind bars while enjoying one's own freedom.

It's a duty of every government to stop the exploitation of animals and to ameliorate their living conditions. We also need more political parties to declare the fight for animal equality their chief aim. Stricter laws are necessary to protect all animals, not only our beloved pets. Educational programs at school and elsewhere are also a vital part of raising people's consciousnesses, as I've already outlined. We have to realize that animals are magnificent, beautiful, and ecologically valuable creatures just like humans, who are worth being saved for their own sake, not only because it's good for people's health to keep at least some wildlife intact.

The coronavirus crisis has vividly shown us that less space for animals means more pandemics for humankind. However, many people don't accept that their own offspring contribute to the diminishment of nature. We all need houses, food, clothes, cars, and other material possessions, which always means fewer animals and places where they can live happily and comfortably, not squeezed together so tightly that diseases move easily and quickly from species to species, eventually affecting humans. FLATTEN THE CURVE is a slogan that is also crucial concerning population growth.

When the Australian Commission for the Human Future (consisting of several scientists) published the survey *Surviving and Thriving in the 21st Century*, they were (surprise!) no cowards, unlike many other people or institutions. The commission emphasized that population growth was a matter to be addressed and tackled. It was the most dangerous threat to humanity in general, they outlined. The nine other risks, they said, were the mass extinction of species, the collapse of ecosystems, the depletion of resources, climate change, air pollution, food shortage, nuclear weapons, pandemics, dangerous new technologies, and misinformation/unwillingness to accept reality.

I always wonder why so few people or the media listen to experts. Is it because we are so used to the old slogan that children are the future? Okay, but by too many children, therefore too many people in the end (we are all born as babies), we destroy this very future everyone is harping on about.

There are ads that proclaim elephants as animals at "high risk" but obviously, for many, only endangered human groups are worth protecting. Have they never heard of Immanuel Kant? Or Christine M. Korsgaard, who is a Kantian and applies his philosophy to animals, e.g., in her book *Fellow Creatures: Our Obligations to the Other Animals*. She outlines that an ape's life, for instance, has absolute value, too—from the ape's perspective. We all need food, shelter, comfort, and freedom from fear, pain, illness—no matter if we are apes or humans or cows. It's indeed our moral duty to care for the animals for the sake of those creatures, without asking ceaselessly what they can do for us. Culture, philosophy, arts—we all have to contribute, even more than we do now, for animal rights to be recognized as universal. Our development as a society depends upon this.

Some say a different way of farming would be enough to satisfy the welfare of animals. Okay, switching to environmentally friendlier farming is one necessary method, but there are still our own unsustainable numbers to take into account. If all the farmland in England and Wales was converted to organic agriculture, greenhouse gas emissions (GHGs) could still rise because the high food demands of the island's population would require using more land abroad.

Talking about land. . . . The global deforestation rate has increased by 43 percent since 2015, although there were some government plans to reverse it in the New York Declaration on Forests of 2014. Most forest is lost because of agriculture—that's why it's high time to think about our population *and* our consumption, since unsustainable growth is just impossible. Restoring nature can only happen if there are not too many of us (which leads to a higher quality of life for humans *and* animals).

Children usually like animals. There are lots of books, movies, and other forms media about our favorite mammals. Yet parents do everything to reduce their numbers in the real world. . . .

Transportation is also a contributor to GHGs. Yet the summer of 2019 showed not fewer plane flights, but a slight increase. Greta Thunberg and her ilk can only achieve so much. Ordinary humans aren't inclined to give up beloved things they grew accustomed to. They like meat, flights, and their cars. Why bother, we think, if we don't have giraffes in 2040 anymore? Who needs them?! The UK National Biodiversity Network's *State of Nature* report of 2019 tells us that a quarter of all mammals and almost half of the U.K.'s bird species are threatened with extinction.

It's immensely sad that conscious people who make personal sacrifices for the sake of the environment nonetheless have to bear the brunt of other people's reckless choices. And as long as capitalism rules the world, no government will take serious action. If we and all the animals die, it appears to them to be no problem, as long as our economy thrives. Something got out of hand decades ago.

The elephant in the room is the human population. And it mustn't be pushed under the carpet, as Dame Jane Goodall reminds us. We all know that humans cause whole populations of animals to crash. But somehow this remains a taboo subject. It's way too late to let this continue. It's vital that more people stop pretending our numbers have nothing to do with our environmental problems. We can recycle our socks off, but if we don't talk about population growth, these efforts will forever be an uphill battle. People and their vast numbers put pressure on the climate, habitats of other species, and resources of all kinds.

So, the world population must be stabilized, as a report of 11,000 scientists confirmed (Ripple, 2020). "When the report was published on November 6, 2019, the BBC had to inform us that the UN still thinks the population issue is "too hot to handle"" (Langdon, 2019). The population increase has a major impact on everything, from emissions to forest clearance—yet so many people can't or don't want to stop pussyfooting around the issue.

Goodall's "colleague" Sir David Attenborough isn't one of them. He received the Indira Gandhi Peace Prize 2019 and is well known for his nature documentaries. Like Goodall, he's one of the patrons of Population Matters, a charity based in the U.K. that's fighting for a sustainable population in order to protect the planet. So many humans are taking over the whole planet, he has said, that there are fewer and fewer wild areas, which also become cramped and encroached upon by roads, buildings, and other infrastructure. "Either we limit our population growth," he said, "or the natural world will do it for us" (Javelosa 2016). Zoonoses will increase, confirms Eric Fèvre (UNEP 2020), professor for veterinary infectious diseases at Liverpool University. This depressing truth has to sink in.

It's a sad fact that the "overpopulation train" overwhelms the best of our environmental and social justice intentions and actions. We're currently consuming resources like fresh water, healthy soil, and forests almost twice as quickly as they can regenerate. If population and consumption trends aren't modified, three Earths would be needed by 2050 to curb resource depletion.

It's not only about the merely physical aspect of our numbers. As Wolfgang Sassin and others note in *Evolutionary Environments: Homo Sapiens—An Endangered Species?*: "Being packed ever more densely and plagued by innumerable interactions, humans are at the point to mutate into mere elements of herds, losing their individual freedom, irrespective of the level of material endowments. [. . .] Next-door neighbours perceived as mere obstacles" (p. 15).

There's lots of talk about the feasibility of somehow managing, of surviving, and of nourishing billions and billions of people and sheltering and clothing them. But what about the quality of life? What about the things and concepts that make us human, and make our miserable lives somehow still worth living, at least in some specific moments? Sassin and others say: "What sense would it make to become an indiscriminate and anonymous element of a mass, in the pursuit of sharing the world with even more of the same?" (p. 120).

Nowadays you have to compete with a large number of people, especially in bigger cities, when you want to get a job or an apartment. Take my home town of Regensburg, for example. This is not a big city, yet there are innumerable sites for innumerable new houses for all those new people who are born every day. Local politicians are well aware of the fact that affordable housing is a top priority. But it's no longer affordable for many citizens. Capitalism and infinite growth in every respect make life hard and unpleasant for many of us.

Tipping points, continue Sassin et al., occur "in herds and swarms as soon as the maneuverability of their members is reduced too much. [. . .] Normally close neighbours contribute to a notion of security and of being safely guarded. This can change in no time into a notion of being threatened by one's direct neighbours. The much-wanted companions then turn into obstacles if not enemies that have to be overcome at any rate (p. 121)."

Peaceful cohabitation is rare among humans, and this is understandable because all those people penned up have different ways of living and expressing themselves when at home, so distress comes naturally. ADULT-ORIENTED BUILDING is a slogan to describe some residences in British Columbia, Canada; and frankly, many non-parents envy the folks lucky enough to live in such a house. Perhaps even a considerable number of parents do, too. In Germany, for instance, it is inconceivable to declare your house childfree. Landlords would face countless lawsuits by enraged parents shouting *Discrimination!* at the top of their lungs.

Why are so many parents always enraged? They have every imaginable privilege, the state fawns over them, they seem to be above criticism—and yet they moan and whine and feel mistreated. . . . One theory is that they have grown so entitled because of the continuing flattery coming in left, right, and center that they can't stand it if only one person doesn't praise them for their wonderful gift to society by reproducing.

Even if we don't criticize, simply ignoring a proud new mother or father can hurt their precious egos considerably, as you can easily find out if you don't smile at their newborn. If you remain facially and or verbally neutral, you've committed a major offense already. Give me a break! If you go one step further and point out that not everyone loves noise—while being on vacation, for example—you'll get the most evil looks that were ever addressed to you.

Yet we know the case of a mother who wants no other children in the building she lives in. She understands people cherishing tranquility and wants it for herself and only her holy offspring is allowed to produce any noise. . . . Unfortunately, more than a few parents act in such a selfish and reckless manner, and it's up to childfree people to make their voices heard. We're no doormats and shouldn't accept being treated as such.

On November 16, 2019, *The Guardian* published an anonymous letter entitled "Letter to . . . Our Neighbours with a Baby," in which a couple complained about the constant noise they had to endure because of their neighbors who chose reproduction. As they pointed out correctly, it's one thing to opt for parenthood, sleepless nights, and so on, but the people next door didn't, and it was callous to make them suffer the same nightmare. This is only possible in such a child-worshipping culture as ours.

To quote the childfree couple: "Her protracted wailing cost us dozens of hours of sleep at a time when our careers were stressful and demanding. It placed an unwelcome strain on our own relationship and soured our enjoyment of our new home. [. . .] The people around you have their own lives to cope with, their own problems that they don't inflict on others. To expect them to share your discomfort is deeply selfish" (Anonymous 2019).

So, once again you sometimes just can't help yourself: It seems as if the parents are so unhappy with their lot that they even enjoy that others suffer because of them. If their sex life goes downhill, why should their neighbors have fun? Maybe because they are completely innocent and have nothing to do with other couples' (wrong) decisions?

But maybe parents just don't think of others, such as their neighbors. They have the most important person in the whole world to look after. It's the most important person *for them*, not for their neighbors, who really shouldn't be expected to put up with anything only because others wanted to contribute to overpopulation. If such innocent people complain, *they* are the bad guys, never the breeders—and this has to change.

It's twice unfair: you are the person harmed, yet you're not even allowed to voice your justified outrage. The signal sent is deeply wrong on so many levels. . . . You are not important. As a breeder, yes, maybe, but your worth as a person is never as important as other people's biological need to procreate.

This is a society that devalues the people those former children become, that favors procreation as a means to perpetuate the status quo eternally—which will never work out, anyway, given the state of our environment. . . . Hopefully, the climate crisis will wake people up. If they don't mind their children living enslaved lives in our capitalist society, maybe they'll mind them having no clean water.

There is no doubt about the fact that herds need guidance. That also applies to human herds. Some might say, *especially* herds consisting of many humans. . . . It's also a widespread truth that collective intelligence is produced by instincts, and not by intellect.

History is full of examples that demonstrate that people usually don't listen to bright individuals. Take Galileo Galilei. Take those warning about the rise of the Nazi party in Germany. Now it's people talking about climate change. Or warning about the rise of the AfD. Or women promoting the idea of fewer new children—in order to save the planet for those already existing. These people are the witches of our time, fit to be burnt alive on the modern stakes—social media. As Sassin et al. comment: "Those who separate themselves in order to develop an independent image of the world are in danger to be expelled" (p. 36).

And you're lucky if you're only expelled, and not physically assaulted or even killed. We've already mentioned the frequent and frankly horrible rape and torture fantasies culminating in bloodshed that can be found online. Especially right-wing young men often have no qualms at all in publishing hate speech, even using their real names, because they know that nothing will happen to them. They express mainstream resentment and there is always safety in numbers. There are just too many of them, which emboldens them to fire away.

My publishing house, for example, had to deal with all the hatred directed at me. The staff told me that they'd received phone calls and emails they had never gotten before. For some time, they were afraid to open parcels! The language used by such trolls shows the brutalization that can be witnessed everywhere. In the past, there were people who didn't refrain from writing nasty letters, but that took time, energy, thought, even money. . . . Nowadays, all they have to do is type: it doesn't cost anything at all, it's instant, and you can get rid of your feelings of frustration and inadequacy quickly and easily. In times when an actress is criticized because of her shoes—in particularly vulgar language—it's no surprise that eco-feminists are really in for it.

You don't have to be a misanthrope, though, to realize that, as Sassin and others point out, "[no] doubt, the number of individuals will have to be limited sooner or later"(p. 14)—if we want a real chance of surviving *at all*. Of course, people accuse you of disliking people and children, of being a gloomy pessimist, but it is their kids who will have to bear the brunt of their reckless behavior.

To use a simple metaphor: if the bus is full, really full, so full that not one more person can board without suffocating one of the others, then the bus driver should be responsible enough to drive past the next bus stop and leave the people waiting there where they are. They'll have to wait for the next bus, which will hopefully arrive ten minutes later and be less crowded. Our planet is the first bus. And there is no second one. So, let's use birth control in order to keep this bus on the road.

"Many of the natural systems, nearly all easily accessible resources, and a largely unpolluted environment, that were available at the beginning of the 20th century for the then living 2 billion, will be consumed within a few decades," say Sassin et al. "There is no pristine creation left as a fallback position" (p. 119). You can't go on exploiting nature, since there will soon be a natural stop because we live on a finite planet that won't survive endless growth. Using simple logic, it should be clear that endless growth is something that can never be. It's a conservative dream, and something less desirable for left-wingers anyway, taking into account that, as Sassin et al. note, "capitalism brought to life the worst forms of slavery" (p. 49). And it will eventually destroy Earth. We can't survive without nature.

Nonetheless, there are too many people who simply don't want to see the obvious. Some might be not that intelligent, but it's frankly shocking how many theoretically sufficiently bright people actively prefer to close their eyes when it comes to climate change and our role in it. It is partly understandable because not everyone wants to cope with mortality, and not everybody can. But in the end, it is not the best or smartest option to ignore impending doom, hoping that it will just disappear if you ignore it long and hard enough.

And so, say Sassin et al., hopes "of a bright and open future clash with an even tighter reality, with a flood of economic crises, environmental instabilities, with failing societies, terrorism and existential competition on a planet that simply turns out to be too small for homo sapiens. Not stable and powerful civilizations are obviously clashing, but fragments and splinters of faltering civilizations are clashing and provide ample evidence of their internal decay" (p. 78).

The internal decay becomes manifest in social media reactions whenever someone so much as mentions overpopulation. You'll be sure to find somebody posting a shitty video about the "myth" of overpopulation, to read hundreds of nasty comments, to come across the brilliant suggestion that this person kill themselves to reduce overpopulation. How immensely witty, congrats! You've just proven that you're not only anti-social but also just plain stupid. It's the main difference we're talking about. Merely existing isn't a crime: nobody can be blamed for having been brought into this crappy world. But actively bringing someone into it? *That* can be considered a crime—against the environment *and* against the new person.

When it comes to suicide prevention, the only guaranteed way to prevent it from happening is to prevent birth. Once born, the risk of trauma, mental illness, crisis, and suicide increases for every individual. The Colombian writer, director, and biologist Fernando Vallejo also encourages people not to repeat the crime committed against them by imposing life. Why bring anyone into this slaughterhouse we've come to die in? he asks. Andy Warhol seconds: Being born is like being kidnapped. And then sold into slavery.

No wonder, as Sassin and others observe, that interconnecting "the brains of billions online inevitably reduces homo sapiens intelligence to crowd intelligence" (p. 85). That can be seen on Facebook, Instagram, and Twitter. Too many people sadly don't realize that globalization, sustainability, and humanity don't go that well together.

Sassin et al. continue: "[Samuel] Huntington's Clash of Civilizations, Norbert Elias's Process of Civilization and in a quite different discipline Wolf Singer's Evolution as a cognitive Process, Nick Bostrom's Superintelligence and many other such oeuvres suggest that we are witnessing a second type of Enlightenment. And nobody can guarantee that the technical means to create new mental—and therefore always virtual spaces—will not end up in systems of dethroning homo culturis and turn back our mental evolution to the ages of dinosaurs" (p. 115). Again, one striking example for that apprehension is the comment section of any online post you can find. There will always be some idiot voicing criminal opinions full of stupidity and hatred.

2.3 The Club of Rome

The Club of Rome, an association of experts from many different countries, was founded in 1968 and regularly publishes ideas for a sustainable future. As early as 1972, the organization's report *Limits to Growth* mentioned population growth, industrialization, resource consumption, and environmental pollution as likely risks of transforming the planet and finally causing a collapse of civilization sometime in the twenty-first century. As Graeme Maxton and Jørgen Randers argue in *Reinventing Prosperity* (2016), programs to step up the fertility rates of Western societies are wrong and stupid; fighting social injustice, unemployment, and climate change are important.

Hence, an absolutely brilliant idea I also presented in my German book *Kinderfrei statt kinderlos* (*Child-Free Instead of Child-Less*): that the Club of Rome award $80,000 to every childfree woman on her fiftieth birthday. The result of my idea? An outcry in Germany, Austria, and Switzerland—as if I had reinvented the wheel! Shouldn't they get all the money? complained the breeders. Why reward people who *don't* contribute to overpopulation and climate collapse? But obviously, the whiners had succeeded in ignoring the Club of Rome's idea before, or just didn't relish being reminded of such a horrible idea.

It's the same sad story over and over again. Parents are highly subsidized everywhere—yet they want more and more. In Germany, education for children and young adults is *completely free*. Well, that's something, isn't it? Somehow, this slips parents' minds—as does the fact that pregnancy and childbirth are completely covered by your health insurance, although the amount per single baby is huge. The list is endless, but parents have managed to convince the public—mainly consisting of parents, sadly—that there's still not enough done for them.

Not many people listened to the Club of Rome, and not many listen to BirthStrike, either. Blythe Pepino thought long and hard about whether to start a family or not—and eventually decided against this project with her partner. Similar to other BirthStrikers, she went public with her decision and named climate change as the first and most important reason to abstain from becoming a mother. Responsible people wonder what their kids would have to live through when they are in their thirties. BirthStrike is quite well-known and several women in the U.K. have joined it. The situation in Germany, however, is somewhat desperate. Here, you get death threats when you talk about this issue openly.

English people wrote to me after they read about me in the U.K. *Sunday Times*: "Verena, you're a leader. Thank you!" they said, or "You touched my heart and mind." Interestingly, British and American journalists were much friendlier and understanding than German or Austrian ones, even if they lived in Germany. One example was Neil King and Gabriel Borrud, journalists based in Cologne, who interviewed me for their podcast *On the Green Fence*. They called remaining childfree for environmental reasons the "ultimate sacrifice," and told me that Gabriel's brother also felt this way.

In summer 2019, statements by Miley Cyrus that she would remain childfree and by Prince Harry that he wouldn't have a big family were received with surprise—and almost every text mentioned the name of the "crazy Bavarian teacher" who had introduced the German audience to such an incredible idea some months before. . . . A very slight shift in perception could be noticed, but the majority in this country unfortunately remained hostile and glued to ancient ideas that won't help the planet at all—on the contrary.

In Germany, we have no *Sydney Morning Herald*, which portrayed childfree couples in 2019, listing two types of reasons: Why contribute to overpopulation, and why force an innocent new creature into such a world? (Fitzsimmons 2019). Nevertheless, even in progressive, relaxed Australia many of the people interviewed preferred to remain anonymous, because they feared negative reaction online or in real life, and this is what makes it all so sad.

It's great when pop stars like Taylor Swift point out that it's slightly rude to ask a woman approaching her thirtieth birthday when she's going to start a family. Women are more than incubators, Swift said in *People* magazine in December 2019. It's not only rude, but also anti-feminist as well. No man of thirty (!) has to endure questions like that. Everyone expects him to enjoy his life till . . . well . . . time will tell *if* he wants to become a father someday or not. We urgently need the same standards for women; we can't accept different expectations any longer. Becoming older isn't a road into irrelevance and decay—and this applies to *men* and *women*.

Yet there are some people in Austria and Germany who also intend to remain childfree for environmental reasons. Some of them were mentioned in an article published on November 26, 2019 in *Die Presse*, Vienna. But they weren't brave enough to give their full name or picture, so they sent a photographer to me. It is hard indeed to hold and defend this view, but it's invaluable to do so!

Switzerland was somehow more advanced. The *Neue Zürcher Zeitung* featured an article about women who didn't want to give birth (one of them wasn't afraid of telling the journalist her name), mentioning my book that had started the whole discussion several months ago. And even though this article was not immensely positive, and rather kind of neutral, at least it lacked the negative attitude expressed by so many others.

"Despite all scientific progress," say Sassin et al., "nearly everybody seems to believe reproduction would be fate, not an act of free will, a property every single individual claims in all other cases without limits" (p. 129). There still are—and not only among religious people—online posts featuring a newborn and a caption that reads: "We are so happy that little Tom came to us." Well, was it the stork that brought him?

Contraception is something we luckily possess in the West. (Many African or Asian women in poor regions of Indonesia or Malaysia, for instance, would love to limit the number of children they give birth to, but sadly can't.) It should also be free. And it should be used. Sassin et al. concur: "With the pill individuality got a new dimension and a new meaning. [. . .] Every pill taken by a woman, irrespective of her individual motivations, has the power to influence the long-term future of mankind more than all investments in armaments, climate, and human rights conventions taken together" (pp. 143, 145). They continue that wealth isn't being blessed with children anymore. Now human labor is substituted by technological devices "that need not be educated laboriously and the efficiency of those devices is not absorbed at a later stage by having to reproduce themselves again" (ibid.).

In some parts of Africa, people still see things differently, but partly because they *are* different. In a documentary about Uganda, one teenage son pointed out to his father, who wanted ever more children—against the will of his wife, who was exhausted by too many pregnancies—that the life he was inflicting on his kids wasn't exactly paradise. He was polite and made lots of sense. He talked about scarce resources, overcrowded mega-cities where young people ended up drugged or unemployed. Let's hope this young man's generation will act accordingly.

Key to reduced birth rates in developing countries are of course education and the empowerment of girls and women. More gender equality, improved healthcare, and better sanitation always help. Mahamadou Issoufou, the president of Niger, has explained that exploding birth rates can be attributed to misinterpreting the Qur'an (Wintour 2019). The more women know about their own body, about feminism, and about the interdependencies of religion and politics, the more likely they are to aim higher than having lots and lots of babies. There are still many women who are unable to choose the number or the time when and where to have children! Everyone knows about horrific consequences, as unwanted pregnancies can end fatally for mothers and infants alike. So, it's great that the British government is going to spend £600 million more on family planning in poor countries (Ford 2019). This is an investment that will really pay off and make many women's lives worth living. Of course, African children use fewer resources than European or North American ones, but looking at this topic from a feminist point of view (cf. Chapter 2) is also outrageous that there are still women who don't have access to contraception in 2022.

There have to be profound changes concerning pension schemes—not only in some African countries but also in the West. Children shouldn't be used to provide for their old parents, one way or the other. They owe us nothing. They didn't ask to be born. It just doesn't work that way: *I brought you here, so I expect you to look after me when I'm old.* This puts lots of pressure on young shoulders and often doesn't function anyway; it's just too simplistic.

Of course, women's empowerment is once again absolutely crucial—not only in this respect, but fundamentally. Education and family planning usually bring birth rates down. There are more than 200 million women worldwide who have problems achieving access to birth control. These women have to get all the help they deserve, ASAP!

It can't be emphasized enough how important the role of the West is. It's absolutely disrespectful—not to mention completely and utterly racist—to point our fingers at Africa and say something along the lines of *If they reduce breeding first, maybe we'll consider having fewer children too.*

Many people—e.g., in the German-speaking part of Europe— just don't know (or pretend not to know) that thirty African kids use as many resources as one western European child (Fitzgerald 2019). If you take a very poor country like Chad, for instance, things get much worse: roughly ninety children living there use what one single western child "needs." This highly embarrassing truth should really make us think about our ecological footprint.

Leafing through the *National Geographic Magazine*, for example, you'll find out that an average Westerner drives around so much that it would be enough to circle the whole planet twenty-five times, drinks 26,000 glasses of milk, eats more than a ton of bananas and two tons of bread, uses 1.8 million liters of water and lots of fuel too. We will also produce sixty-four tons of trash each. Is anyone surprised that our planet is dying? The same magazine informs us in June 2019 that one million species face the risk of extinction—due to human activities.

Many environmental organizations do everything to save the planet, but only one aspect is often missing. We would be very happy if they had the courage to finally acknowledge that the most important contribution to saving Earth that each individual can make is not to procreate.

Allison Lance from the Galapagos Preservation Society is brave enough to state the obvious: "Is it smart to bring a kid into this down-spiraling world? I am sick of hearing: My baby could grow up to change the world! Bullshit. There are already a lot of people trying to bring change, but there are too many people consuming, using resources, living without thinking or feeling. Bringing a child into the world is selfish, dangerous, and totally irresponsible" (Kemmerer 2011, p. 146).

Yet there are billions of people who just don't care and reproduce as if everything was okay. Do they never think of the future these children are going to have? They seem "to overlook that scarce resources, climate change, or the collapse of big ecosystems will force them to stoke negative emotions and thereupon line up and fight against each other in order to survive" (Sassin et al., 2018, p. 146).

Philosopher Thomas Hobbes got that one right in the seventeenth century. *Homo homini lupus est* ("a man is a wolf to another man") as well as *Bellum omnium contra omnes* ("the war of all against all") are famous quotes and often used to highlight the writer's misanthropy. One should be careful before judging those who are really far-sighted.

A simple method would be to limit the passengers on Ark Earth. As Sassin et al. state: "What is badly needed in this 21st century, however, is a strategy to organize the controlled reduction of global populations, [. . .] despite the archaic drive of homo sapiens to unlimited biological reproduction. [. . .] It needs a narrative other than collective efforts to control climate. [. . .] The narrative can and must relieve the anxiety caused by ever more humans that appear as the very human threat. It must be transformed into the hope to be able to control human reproduction successfully and sustainably" (p. 160).

Indeed, if there are too many of us competing in every single aspect of everyday life, extreme pressure and stress will be the result and only the ones who are very robust and tough will survive. But what about the dreamers and thinkers, who will only be hindered and exhausted? Overpopulated cities lose their attractiveness, character is crowded out, as an Australian architect puts it.

Speaking of Australia, there seems to be some hope. Former New South Wales Premier Bob Carr openly talks about population policy, which is needed in Australia. (Yes, as everywhere in the world! But especially in industrial countries.) Mr. Carr is also the patron of Sustainable Population Australia (SPA), which has a website that contains lots of interesting information. No wonder there were signs saying GROWTH FOR GROWTH'S SAKE IS THE IDEOLOGY OF A CANCER

CELL OR FACTS IGNORED DON'T CEASE TO EXIST during Australian climate demonstrations.

SPA has no problem pointing out the obvious: the coal mining companies, usually subject to so much criticism, are not the core problem. There is demand for the product, so someone will produce it. Demand is generated by us, the people, the consumers. Blaming the system, its politicians, and companies alone is just copping out. And it achieves little in addressing the problem of climate change.

SPA also shared the Australian politician Kelvin Thomson's speech about the threat of overpopulation from 2019, and it's really sad that it's still so relevant today; indeed, even more so. Thomson mentioned global warming, food crises, water shortages, housing affordability, overcrowded cities, traffic congestion, species extinction, collapsing fisheries, increasing prices, trash, terrorism, and war—each and every problem is fueled by population growth (see Thomson 2016). An example for traffic congestion is the increase of weekly commuting time, which is much higher than in 2002, when the average was 3.7 hours. In 2017, it was already 4.5 hours. And it doesn't stop. This phenomenon isn't restricted to Australia, by the way.

David Wallace-Wells published *The Uninhabitable Earth* in 2019, describing how today's kids and teenagers are sure to live through a dramatically declining quality of life.

This is capitalism, this is how it works. . . . As many people as possible, buying and consuming; but nobody really cares, their physical and mental health—minor details.

If people go on breeding like they do now, every problem will become more severe, that's for sure. And it is not only trash and plastic we're talking about; we're talking absolutely vital resources too. But it's easy to blame politicians. *They should come up with a solution.* Why help the planet yourself if others can conveniently do that?

But children are just so wonderful, aren't they, this sacrifice is just too much! Well, why does it always have to be your own child, then? Why not adopt? Why breed when the shelters are full? The suspicion arises that it has to be someone with your own genes. So, it's pure hypocrisy to claim *it's about kids, I just like them so much*. No! It's about *you*.

But here's news: if everyone thought like that and popped out babies left, right, and center, the planet would have come to an end already. So, people who reproduced have no right at all to attack the childfree. Far from it! They have the duty to be thankful. We fine childfree folk could easily behave just like them, reproducing recklessly, not considering other living beings, thinking solely about passing on our oh-so-special genes. So please stop bullying the people who refrain from procreation because of your children. There may be some for whom this sacrifice is easy, but for some it's not and they really don't deserve scorn or hatred because of their noble goal: saving the planet for those who already exist. It's one thing not to be grateful, but doing the opposite is often just criminal and always incredibly stupid.

One example is the invitation of the "heartless teacher" to a panel discussion about our global species extinction in September 2019. The great physician and environmental activist who organized this event got hate mail as soon as it became known whom he had invited. During the discussion, the atmosphere was not always friendly. People simply dislike hearing facts that don't suit them. Well, sorry again: not breeding is by far the most important thing you can do for the climate and the planet.

After the event, a member of an animal protection party came up to me and expressed his delight. We also took photos. Posting them on Facebook cost the poor guy dearly. . . . Several people unfriended him instantly! Not to mention the usual hate speech typical of such people. Those are the ones that even manipulate their own children (while insinuating that I'm doing that). They incite them to be spiteful toward people whose opinion differs from their own; they actively promote aggressive behavior and negative attitudes (mostly a combination of racist, sexist, and homophobic tendencies). It can't be emphasized enough how stupid and anti-social some parents can be; on the other hand, there are brilliant parents who share this (scientific) view (we are talking about facts here) wholeheartedly. Maybe it's just a question of intelligence: parents with brains realize that protecting the planet might be a good thing. They also seem capable of realizing another aspect: that I'm never talking about people who already exist, but about those we could theoretically give birth to—solely because we are owners of reproductive organs.

There is another interesting dividing line. It's not only parents who attack me because of my attitude, some childless women do also. And this is extremely sad. When I took part in a working dinner, this division became crystal clear: almost immediately there were two parties. The host, Friedrich von Borries, a well-known architect and writer, had invited twelve guests to talk about living without consequences—if such a life was any possibility at all. There were also two winegrowers and two cooks, who made this evening really outstanding. A small film team recorded the event, which took place in a museum near Vienna, on October 18, 2019. Friedrich had asked four activists as special guests: a priest who'd fought for German reunification, a literary scholar, a businesswoman promoting sustainability, and myself, "BirthStrike Verena." A lady working for a radio station was also present.

We got to talking and as soon as "my" topic came up, one part of the oblong table we were sitting at became aggressive. The businesswoman, a mother of three, emerged as their spokesperson, and soon accused me of dominating the conversation—which was simply not true. She herself was quite domineering and couldn't stand that *another woman* talked as much as she did. She didn't mind long monologues delivered by the priest. . . .

Even more disappointing was the woman next to her, also in her fifties, the literary scholar. She showed an incredible stubbornness and didn't like my point of view at all, "although" she herself was child*less*. And this is another reason why the distinction between child*free* and child*less* is so important.

It wasn't the first time that childless women, especially around forty or fifty years old, completely lost it when confronted with me and everything I stand for. They can't get over the fact that I can reject such a great "present/power" or whatever it is in their opinion that childbearing confers. These women are usually single and envy my status as a married woman, which is absolutely unbelievable. Is it the backlash's fault? One of them owned up to this feeling in a tête-à-tête: yes, she wanted a husband like mine, and then she would give birth to two children. Great! I was too amused to be shocked by the subtext of why I needed a hubby at all, if I didn't intend to breed anyway. "We *do* own ovaries, so let's use them," she said, "especially if you have a wonderful partner with whom to start a family. It's a sacrilege not to."

Luckily, there was the host's sister, who has several children, but (surprise!) she was on my team. She pointed out that I was her counterpart, and that she was glad there were childfree people—otherwise the planet would be dead already, if everyone had as many kids as she did. She got that right and at least she didn't deny her mega-footprint. She added that one of her daughters might consider me an icon. *If there's enough time left*, I thought, but didn't say it because this mother was so lovely and friendly and the complete opposite of the hostile faction down the table. . . . Of course, she's egotistic, breeding several times when the environment is as threatened as it is now. Of course, she's not a feminist (she admitted that openly, she called herself a housewife), yet she behaved in a way that was absolutely acceptable—especially in comparison to the two older women. But she's intelligent and realizes, exactly like my friends who are mothers and fathers, that the childfree do them a great favor, that parents need the childfree!

Her response also disproves the notion that I play parents off against non-parents. Absolutely not. Intelligent parents grasp the idea of living childfree and the value of this decision for them and their children, first and foremost. Only extremely stupid and inconsiderate parents want everyone else to pop out as many babies as possible too.

Others understand that there are people like me, who prefer a working, happy relationship without the strains of parenthood attached to it. There are thousands of single parents in every country, which alone is proof that kids have a negative effect on couples. Nick Hornby's novel *About a Boy* (1998) is still sadly relevant over two decades since its publication: there is SPAT (Single Parents Alone Together) and there is the main character, Will—and roughly twenty women. . . .

In every country, single parents are overwhelmingly female—what a surprise! Somehow, it's almost in every case the mother who keeps the child/children when a couple splits. The father enjoys the single life again or sets up camp with another woman. This aspect shouldn't be neglected when pondering the question of procreation. We all know how hard the fate of single motherhood is, and not only financially. It's not only Fiona, the thirty-eight-year-old mom of Marcus in Hornby's novel, who tries to commit suicide.

2.4 Extinction Rebellion and Others of That Ilk

Extinction Rebellion, allegedly fighting against climate change, seems like an esoteric cult, appealing to people's emotions rather than to their minds. Often, they cry and meditate together. Fittingly, the leaders have built groups in a hierarchic way, so it's not really a grassroots movement anyway. They also conducted surveys quizzing participants about other memberships, political activities, and so on.

Extinction Rebellion, which was founded in England by capitalists, is furthermore not really against nuclear power plants, sexism, or racism. Well, maybe they just don't want to exclude anyone. Fittingly, Roger Hallam, one of the founders, even calls the Holocaust just *another fuckery in human history* (Connolly & Taylor 2019)!

Extinction Rebellion claims that it fights for life, for people— this sounds a bit like a pro-lifer's agenda. . . . It's not genuinely a feminist, left-wing movement. The leaders never say that they want to combat exploitation. Well, no surprise there, as they are supported by a new class of capitalists who produce "ecologically friendly" products. They simply want to sell their products, and if a bit of mass hysteria helps to achieve that, so be it.

Helping the environment has been a (theoretical) goal of many political parties since the 1970s, but not much has happened. Man-made catastrophes occur daily everywhere and they always hit the poorest countries first. Yet the politicians in the West act almost cynically. It is and always will be economy first, ecology second (or not at all). . . . It seems to be forbidden to change something radically. But radical change is necessary; we don't have enough time to make only small contributions to save the planet, they just don't suffice anymore! Fridays For Future and several other organizations do realize that there is no planet B, yet they behave as if there was endless time, talking about their kids and even grandchildren! How can one be so blind? Maybe it's their youth. We don't expect them to grasp the concept of anti-natalism (feminism is out anyway), but "their" topic is protecting the environment. Is it so hard to understand that more and more people produce more and more waste, need places to live, clothes to wear, food to eat (maybe even meat), vehicles to get from A to B (cars, planes, and so on)? Environmentalism taken seriously can only result in rejecting reproduction and capitalism.

By not breeding you don't produce a new consumer—that's what every grown-up leftist can do. Because as soon as you do exist, you have to consume at least some goods in order to stay alive. Only very few people manage to live self-sustainingly. It's not your fault you exist, but it's definitely your "fault" if you decide to bring another person into this capitalist, rotten world. . . .

In one interview, a journalist from Greenpeace (!) asked me if the idea of BirthStrike could work over time. Well, if you think that there's not enough time for long-term methods, then why on Earth would you bring a new human being— who'll have a horrible life at the age of, let's say, eight or nine—into such a world? Isn't it sufficiently cruel for us to face such bleak prospects? Do we really have to inflict this on innocent new people?

Our predicament is definitely self-inflicted and it's actually too late anyway. It was in the 1970s when more resources were consumed than could be regenerated (cf. Casey 2019). So we should educate people, promote family planning, and empower women around the world. (According to the United Nations, the number of people who need humanitarian aid is expected to reach a record 168 million in 2020 and over 200 million in 2022, and this estimate was made in December 2019, before the pandemic.) Many women (and men) who do not want a large family have no access to contraception. This has to change.

And of course, governments should encourage people to have fewer children, not more. Having children was a personal decision decades ago but in 2022, it's a decision with ethical implications for all of humankind and the world we live in. Our per capita consumption multiplied by the vast number of people on the planet clearly leaves no other choice: there needs to be a much lower birth rate. It's people who are responsible for climate change. A growing population counteracts the positive effects of other important climate actions, and choosing small families is crucial if we want to achieve something.

That's why Population Matters used a seven-meter-inflatable baby to convey this message to people in London's Parliament Square on November 29, 2019. The baby's shirt had this text on it: GUESS MY WEIGHT IN CO_2. . . .

Dangerous and harmful ideologies that put growth (for growth's sake) first have to be abandoned.

Greta Thunberg is from Sweden. Why does she not listen to Frank Götmark, a great professor (animals, ecology, wildlife diversity) teaching there? He organizes the International Science Festival, for example, informing everyone that I=PAT is our biggest problem: Impact = Population x Affluence x Technology. He is also part of the Intergovernmental Panel on Climate Change, which explicitly states that overpopulation and overconsumption are mainly responsible for the problems our environment is having. One of his many activities is Project Syndicate, where he publishes articles (by himself and other experts), like "The World and the UN Must Reduce Population Growth" (Götmark & Maynard 2019).

There are many institutions mentioning the main problem; another example is the National Centre for Climate Restoration (Breakthrough) in Melbourne, Australia. David Spratt and Ian Dunlop are two scientists working there who also emphasize that we must tackle the biggest of all problems too—instead of ignoring it.

The British economist Adair Turner contributed the article "In Praise of Demographic Decline" (Turner 2019), and many other magazines like *Science Nordic* or *Science Daily* don't hesitate to call a spade a spade. There are people like Jonathan Franzen, who wrote *What If We Stopped Pretending?* (Franzen 2019), or BBC environmental expert Matt McGrath (McGrath 2019). But many prefer listening to teenagers like Greta or Emma Lim, the young Canadian who initiated #NoFutureNoChildren, where youngsters post sentimental stories that they would love to be a mom, but sadly, the environment has several problems. These teens might be cute, but their naivety can't be denied. Lots of experts agree that the climate collapse can't be prevented anymore, yet they think they can pressurize governments in this way "to fix the planet," so they can have kids. States and capitalism need reproduction, that's how they function. Lim's pledge also lacks feminist elements.

3

FEMINISM

The childfree movement started back in the 1970s—of course, this period being feminism's heyday. Two famous childfree organizations were established during this epoch, the National Organization for Non-Parents and No Kidding!

The Merriam-Webster Online Dictionary tells us that the term *childfree* appeared for the first time in 1901. Figures! It was in 1903 when British suffragette Emmeline Pankhurst founded the Women's Social and Political Union: they organized hunger strikes in the U.K. and countless other peaceful activities, and in 1918 they succeeded in their campaign—women over thirty were allowed to vote. In the U.S., white women got the right to vote in 1920, women of color in 1965.

The French feminist Simone de Beauvoir wrote in her book *Le Deuxième Sexe* (1949) about the different parenting styles applied to girls and boys. Females, she argued, were encouraged to play with dolls and find joy in activities preparing them for their future roles as housewives and mothers. Her oeuvre was quite influential and paved the way for Second Wave Feminism—the real thing.

There were lots of struggles left to be fought: in the 1960, for example, a woman who pursued a career needed her husband's approval. In the 1970s, women didn't need that anymore if they wanted to work. In 1976, the Hite Report was published, a study by Shere Hite, showing that every third woman didn't reach orgasm when having sex with her husband. Women fought for their right to climax—and to abort.

The glory days of the 1970s featured icons like Gloria Steinem, Andrea Dworkin (one of my favorite radical feminists, famous for her fierce fights against pornographers), Kate Millett, and Phyllis Chesler. The latter one wrote extensively about motherhood and didn't seem to see a discrepancy between feminism and fulfilling the core imperative for women in every patriarchal society: giving birth.

Gloria Steinem is absolutely brilliant and a real role model for every woman when she points out that when the pill came along, we were able to give birth—to ourselves. True, there are some side effects and it's high time that more research is done to provide a suitable alternative for men (why should women, who can become pregnant only on some days per month, risk several severe consequences when men, whose fertility is a problem every day, could also contribute to contraception?). But Ms. Steinem emphasizes the great liberty of being childfree and celebrates it as a genuine feminist concept. No wonder the childfree movement coincided with the global Second Wave Feminism.

Third Wave (starting in the 1980s) and Fourth Wave Feminisms are somewhat diluted versions of what real feminism should look like: a fight to liberate women from traditional roles, such as homemakers, mothers, prostitutes, low-income-workers, in order to set free their individuality and strength, to empower them properly. These feminisms should be about destroying the cage, not painting it a nicer color to ameliorate the situation of living behind bars.

In the U.S., there are several great role models for childfree women, such as Oprah Winfrey, who told *People* magazine on October 9, 2019, why she never married or had kids. She also said she didn't have any regrets. This is also what actresses Betty White and Helen Mirren confirmed. White, being over ninety, even said her old age and good health were due to her childfree life. Physical, psychological, and economic wellbeing enhance your chances to have a long, happy life. . . . White is an example of someone who reveals myths about loneliness in your dotage as exactly that: myths. A German study found that childfree senior citizens aren't lonelier than their peers who are parents (and often grandparents). Many of the latter live in retirement homes, neglected by their offspring.

Childfree people have more and, more importantly, richer and deeper friendships they have cultivated over decades, and this is what counts. It's becoming more and more popular to share an apartment with other seniors, helping each other out.

Journalist Meghan Murphy wrote a brilliant article in *The Spectator* in September 2019 in response to Fridays For Future (although she has a more general point here). Called "No, I Will Not Listen to the Children," she said: "In a culture that routinely ignores, denigrates, erases, and disrespects older women, tossing them aside the moment they are no longer fuckable or able to reproduce the species, being ordered to 'listen to youth' strikes me as not only a slap in the face, but a call to ignorance" (Murphy 2019).

Gertrud Backes and Wolfgang Clemens are two of Germany's leading scholars in social gerontology. They have published several books about the challenges and possibilities of ageing. They confirm intuitive notions of the childfree: If you don't need all your time and energy for your kids, you can invest more in significant friendships based on real common interests—and not on the mere coincidence that there are couples/people who also have children. How many mothers suffer silently because of their kid's playdate's stupid parent? It's much more enjoyable to choose your own friends and engage in activities you both adore. These meaningful friendships between childfree people often endure decades—unlike those loose bonds of parents, which dissolve as soon as the kids graduate.

This is equally true for grandparents. Basically, they show the same egoism/narcissism as parents, when they care for their kids' kids and aren't interested in any other children. The same phenomenon can be stated if you look at the range of topics you can discuss properly with the individuals in question. Parents often have a rather narrow, superficial selection of issues relevant to them and this is also the case with many grandparents. Of course, it's clear that the expenditure of time is always an aspect: When are you supposed to read when several little beings needing constant attention surround you?

I personally know lots of older folks. Many grandmothers enjoy caring for their grandkids, thereby also helping their own children. Fine. In conversations you quickly notice that they often aren't the most informed creatures roaming the earth. . . . Not because they are stupid or not interested, but apart from sleeping, chores, care work, etc. they have only so much time and energy left.

Childfree seniors, on the contrary, are often very well informed, write letters to the editor, are politically active, have more friends and acquaintances outside the family, and do more for society as a whole—not only for some consanguineous individuals. In general, they see the bigger picture. (Of course, there are always exceptions, one way or the other.)

Researchers like Backes have found that older single ladies are more mobile. When a whiff of loneliness hit them (which was not often the case), they coped quickly and well. They saw how hard certain family problems were for their peers and appreciated their freedom. Sixty percent of the seniors in Backes' book said they saw family as some kind of minefield, where potential threats lurked around every corner. One misguided step could get you into big trouble, often smoldering for decades (Backes & Clemens 2013).

Nonetheless, acquaintances turn to the childfree seniors when they need help (rather than to men they know), because caring seems a typically female thing to enjoy. . . . So why are these results often ignored or downplayed, only to lure young women into the motherhood trap?

There is also a subgroup of older mothers who are glad when their children don't make the same mistake. They don't even have to participate in Regretting Motherhood; it's enough to realize that times have changed and that procreation isn't such a good idea anymore in 2022. These are mothers who didn't have a real choice when they became pregnant but are happy now that their daughters can enjoy everything they couldn't.

Sadly, many mothers over fifty nudge their daughters in the direction of motherhood. Childfree women write to me telling me that they don't know how to break their decision to their moms.

In 2015, the movie *Trainwreck* was released, starring comedian Amy Schumer, who also wrote the script. In the beginning, everything seems quite cool—for instance, the heroine's lack of enthusiasm when her conservative sister announces her pregnancy. Unfortunately, the heroine, who's called Amy, admits that, in the end, she simply envied her sister. . . . Is it really such a "natural" thing to do, longing for your own small white-bread family, if you have a myriad of other options?

In the movie, Amy realizes that she was wrong, that a stable relationship is something you need—desperately—and she had problems with that at first because of some unresolved issues with her dad. Well! Not every woman who is not in favor of monogamy has childhood trauma. Most of them simply want to enjoy their freedom, just like men.

The sad thing about this movie is that it's from the twenty-first century, not from the nineteenth. If you think of Henry James' novel *The Bostonians*, which is about Olive Chancellor, a feminist fighting for women's liberation, it's not that surprising that her young friend

Verena Tarrant finally betrays feminism by choosing Basil Ransom, a very conservative man.

At the time when Henry James wrote this book, it was clear and understandable that he would portray women in such a way. Furthermore, he was a man. . . . Kate Chopin and Edith Wharton offer more progressive female characters in their works: for instance, Edna in Chopin's *Awakening*, who even prefers suicide over losing her autonomy.

Yet it's sad to witness when Verena gives up everything for Basil, who could be called a masculinist *avant la lettre*. And it's even more depressing when a successful woman writes screenplays like *Trainwreck* centuries later. What makes her do such a thing? The knowledge that stories like this always sell? Amy is considered unfeminine when she doesn't want to cuddle with her latest sexual partner (and this is only one of many clichés and stereotypes this movie sadly perpetuates).

Luckily, there are several books about female autonomy and sexual fulfillment. Rebecca Chalker's very successful *The Clitoral Truth* (2000), for example, is a winning combination of anatomy, history, and self-help. Who knew that six- to eight-thousand afferent nerves are in the clitoris? Its structure is actually quite complex: it's not only the *glans clitoridis*, there also are the *praeputium clitoridis*, the *corpus*, the *crura clitoridis*, and the *corpora cavernosa clitoridis*. It's nice to know the different parts of one of our greatest assets.

If you find the Latin terminology awkward, you can refer to your *Rubyfruit Jungle*—like the title of Rita Mae Brown's famous novel, first published in 1973, when feminism was becoming all the rage. Those were the days when women didn't have to shave. . . .

All of Brown's early books are absolutely brilliant, especially *In Her Day* (1976), which features a lesbian couple divided more than just by a huge age difference, or *Six of One* (1978), where the relationship of Ramelle and Celeste inspired me immensely. (I even dreamed about these two characters when I was a teenager.) Well, nowadays I'd dream about many of the female characters in *Batwoman*, I guess, but queer super heroines didn't exist back then. There were some soap operas regularly featuring gay and or lesbian couples, but it was all quite artificial and often just a poor imitation of the heterosexual relationships that were in the center of the plot anyway.

Of course, the internet changed a lot in this respect. Now you can binge-watch *Queer Duck* (currently on Showtime in the U.S.) and his friends Oscar Wildcat, Openly Gator, and Bi-Polar Bear. There are not only adult animated comedy web television series such as *Queer Duck*, but also countless movies, series, docusoaps, documentaries, and amateur videos, which is a good thing. Queer people generally don't feel alienated anymore and if they want to, they can spend all their leisure time in this universe (which can certainly cause other problems).

This situation is better than it is for childfree people. There's not so much around for them, which speaks to the reason for this book. Of course, there's a myriad of cultural products that feature childfree individuals, but the topic as such isn't prominent or even an issue. It's just the way it is.

In mainstream movies or television, pro-natalism is omnipresent. US productions in particular really rub it in. I imagine it must be hard for a person raised in a single-parent household. Every second movie is about a person looking for daddy. Take *Father Figures* (2017), where two twin brothers over forty travel up and down the country searching for the guy who had sex with their mom in spring 1975. One of the boys is relaxed and pretty cool and is happy to have a great mother; his brother, on the other hand, is obsessed by the absent figure and has made his own life (and that of his son!) hell. Why is *dad* so important, whereas mothers are often taken for granted?

Big Daddy (1999) offers a similar case: Adam Sandler is every kid's dream daddy, allowing them to wear whatever they like, eat, play, and watch whatever they fancy. So many father–son constellations and not really much cool stuff about mothers and daughters.

For childfree feminists, these movies can be annoying, although most of the moviegoing public appears to find them immensely funny, with nothing remarkable about the father–son relationship being the pivot of the whole film, or the jokes about pissing on walls/doors/in pots/on other people, etc. Is this really so amusing? I'm not inhibited at all, but as part of the group who can't pee her name in the snow that easily, these jokes are rather lost on me.

These are the means by which phallocentrism is perpetuated. It's not only the French director Patrick Jean, who produced *La Domination Masculine* in 2009 as well as other great documentaries showing mainstream male dominance, who points out that frequent phallic references are considered normal in our everyday life, be it in France, the U.S., or Germany. Another part of his feminist engagement is his foundation of Zéromacho (French feminist Florence Montreynaud wrote a book about it with the same title), which is an organization of men against prostitution. Zéromacho has achieved some successes, and is one reason why France introduced the Nordic Model, which decriminalizes prostituted people and criminalizes sex buyers in order to put an end to instituted male violence toward women. (Yes, I know there is also a small minority of men who work as prostitutes, but their clients are still mostly men. The reasons are the same. I know a Romanian, now forty, who sold his body when he was fourteen out of sheer desperation and need for money.) Abolitionism, instead of painting a cage golden, is the radical feminist approach to prostitution, which is always harmful to women.

Nowadays, it's a scandal when women don't shave. Letting your hair grow naturally makes you an unkempt woman. There are a few stars in the U.S. who sometimes appear with more natural body hair than the norm allows—which gets them attention, indeed.

But as French novelist Éric Reinhardt writes, it's somewhat cheeky of some Americans, who imposed those strict shaving standards for women all over the world, to be *au naturel* now. He makes a connection between carefully planned American cities and the trimming of pubic hair. Unfortunately, as he writes in his *Comédies françaises*, most French women have adopted this way of presenting themselves. He adores natural hair on the whole female body, comparing it to France's beautiful, naturally developed towns and cities.

British Novelist Fay Weldon could write in the 1970s that women with unshaved legs were supposed to be more passionate. Those were the times. . . . Now there are hardly any women under seventy who don't shave their legs.

Leslie Kern writes in *Feminist City* that we need alternative spaces for women. They don't have to be mapped out in advance—although they can be—but we have to perceive and encourage them. This is also true for animals, by the way. We can't ruin their spaces by covering every inch in concrete. It will be interesting to see how the COVID lockdown policies and their consequences provide this opportunity.

There is a feminist impetus in Rebecca Chalker's book about the clitoris, too, which makes it outstanding. Unfortunately, there are some pseudo- or even anti-feminist publications going around, such as Katja Lewina's work *Sie hat Bock* (2020), or "She's Up For It," for instance. The Russian claims to empower women, but as someone who writes articles for *Playboy*, it's no wonder that she somewhat undermines women's autonomy. Of course, there are even more horrible books, which really focus on how to turn girls and women into perfect sex objects for men, but I'm not going to talk about those. Many influencers and products of our popular entertainment industry also contribute to a severe loss of female self-esteem. If you're wondering how to perform perfect blowjobs instead of thinking about your own pleasure, something's definitely wrong.

Feminism for women that aims at their genuine freedom is radical feminism; anything else is grooming and molding women until they fit patriarchal standards.

A strikingly sad example is E.L. James' *Fifty Shades of Grey*—one of popular literature's greatest hits in the last decade. Of course, it's fiction, unlike most of the other books mentioned so far, but what does it tell us about a society, if so many women buy and enjoy a novel whose only content is the psychological and sexual degradation of a female character by a rich, spoiled young man? It takes someone like Rebecca Solnit to state that obedience and subjugation are not empowering, and that the alleged playfulness of it all doesn't make things less ugly.

"Housewife porn," some critics have labeled it. The book is poorly written, it isn't erotic at all, and it is indeed boring porn, putting the woman in the inferior position in every respect. Finally, the heroine ends up becoming a mother. This is an almost paradigmatic version of the whore/saint dichotomy.

If the "sluts" are lucky, a nice sex-buyer will show some mercy and "save" them. . . . Thai women come to mind, ordered by rich Europeans or Americans as live-in housekeepers and sex slaves. Usually, these men also impregnate them. I personally know a prostitute whose dream is to stop working and settle down with one of the nice guys and start a family, being a housewife. When you are young, you are a sex object; later you are a mother. Are there no other roles?! Why are these two so persistently attractive to women in general, but also to writers, politicians, and so on?

This anti-feminist backlash is especially sad, as so many great activists in the past and present fought for an amelioration of the situation for women all over the world. The suffragettes risked their lives for women who don't appreciate this sacrifice.

Around 1800, even the German philosopher Georg Wilhelm Friedrich Hegel wrote about the clitoris, and while several scholars presume that Hegel's intention was to ridicule the female body/sexuality, others claim he's a proto-feminist.

In 2020, Kate Elizabeth Russell wrote about abuse in her novel *My Dark Vanessa*. However, she managed to add some disturbingly anti-feminist features and attitudes. Vanessa witnesses what happens to another victim of Jacob Strane, the teacher who abused her; she is in the eye of a shitstorm, including the "usual" rape and murder threats. Yet Vanessa doesn't react empathically. Instead, slut-shaming is only condemned if she, Vanessa, is the victim; otherwise she indulges in it herself: a classmate is wearing a top only "sluts" wear; a young female teacher she is jealous of (. . .) is called fat several times, etc.

Well, if the author tells *The Guardian* journalist Fiona Sturges that she told her husband "I'll move wherever you get a job, just don't expect me to bring in money," that tells you something (Sturges 2020).

3.1 Happiness

"Comparing couples with and without children, researchers found that the rate of the decline in relationship satisfaction is nearly twice as steep for couples who have children than for childless couples"— or in my words, childfree couples.

These sage words appear in an article for *The Guardian*—written by Matthew D. Johnson, professor of psychology and director of the marriage and family studies laboratory at SUNY Binghamton (Johnson 2016).

The "belief that having children will improve one's marriage is a tenacious and persistent myth among those who are young and in love," Johnson continues. And let's face it, this is a disaster! Many relationships could be saved if this myth was finally debunked.

Lots of studies confirm that couples without children report more romantic bliss (cf. Dickinson 2018). For example, Jennifer Glass from the University of Texas and Robin Simon (Wake Forest University) compared lots of couples, and found that nonparents revealed higher levels of well-being than those adults with kids. (In the U.S., parents were twelve percent less happy than childfree people.)

People are confronted with such myths all the time. It will never stop. Once you are a parent, others—usually those with larger families—seem to bring up most often a certain question: *When are you going for the second one?* Nota bene: *When*, not even *Are you?*

In 2013, Lauren Sandler published *One and Only: The Freedom of Having an Only Child and the Joy of Being One*, which clears up several persistent stereotypes. Only children are often more gifted, generous, better at making new friends, among other qualities, than kids with siblings. Yet many clichés about only children never die.

In his 2019 book *Happy Ever After: Escaping the Myths of the Perfect Life*, Paul Dolan, a professor of behavioral science at the London School of Economics, shows evidence that the happiest—and healthiest—subgroup in our society are unmarried, childfree women. It has long been known that *somehow* men profit more from marrying than women, although there are enough myths out there to perpetuate the conviction that you're lacking something if you're not married—as a *woman*.

Sian Cain writes about this phenomenon in *The Guardian*[1] (Cain 2019) and mentions that although some people suspect the results of Dolan's study, the majority still cling to old-fashioned ideas. Hence the subtitle of Cain's article: "Behavioral scientist Paul

---

1   Sian Cain: "Women Are Happier Without Children or a Spouse, Says Happiness Expert," *The Guardian*, May 25, 2019, https://www.theguardian.com/lifeand-style/2019/may/25/women-happier-without-children-or-a-spouse-happiness-expert.

Dolan says traditional markers of success no longer apply." Exactly. Parenthood is a tradition that's hard to break. But it's definitely worth trying, because otherwise many women will continue to fall into the same traps as their mothers, grandmothers, and all those women before them.

The article even says that unmarried women live longer. It's up for debate if you really *want* to become that old, but many people do, and maybe they would take this feature into account when they contemplate whether to start a family—or not. This information has to be spread more widely so that people can make an informed choice.

An unmarried, childfree woman is stereotyped as the *crazy old cat lady*, a trope widely popularized by *The Simpsons* cartoon series. Why do people in Europe and the Americas tend to attribute pets, especially cats, to senior women? Why do such expressions or words like *spinster* still exist? The idea behind these terms is a combination of misogyny and ageism. Some people really think older women without husbands/kids are so lonely that they almost automatically adopt lots of kittens. Cats allegedly are stubborn and independent, like these women. . . ! Maybe there are worse stereotypes than this one.

Let's not forget the many senior female citizens who own cats but are neither feminists nor childfree; my own grandmother, who died several years ago, was one of them. Then there are those who'd love to have pets, but can't, due to allergies, or inappropriate housing, or insufficient finances, etc. These pet-less people are pitied by some, although there are also those who claim that pets are only a substitute for children. This may be true for a small minority, but not for the large part of pet "owners."

One such pet owner explained to me when I interviewed her on this topic, that she considered her dog rather like a kind of anti-child. She absolutely didn't want to have kids but adored pets. Enraged parents challenged her: If she really was anti-natalist, wasn't it bad for her dog to be born? *What about the ecological footprint of this dog? He eats meat!* The woman under attack had great answers: Her dog was from a shelter; nobody bred him. And she gave him vegan food. The dog was in good shape and her vet confirmed that the dog's food seemed to agree with him perfectly. (It's worth noting that dogs need large amounts of protein and carefully balanced "vegan diets" to avoid vitamin deficiencies, fatty and amino acid deficiencies, and other digestive issues from plant fibers. If you're considering turning your dog vegan, purchase from companies specializing in animal-free pet food, such as Because Animals and Wild Earth.)

Back to the *cat lady*: a cat is supposed to be *the* animal for lesbians, as you can see in detective stories written by Rita Mae Brown and others. It was women's bodies and their fluids when Brown was young, now it's only cats and dogs, some argue. Would that be such a crime?

Homophobia is a criterion we should never forget if we talk about "out" lesbians. Yes, there are several very popular ones, such as talkshow host Ellen DeGeneres and soccer player Megan Rapinoe, for instance, yet there are still lots of angry men who want to beat and rape them. . . . The *crazy old cat lady* is seldom a woman who doesn't get a man, but one who doesn't want one, be it because she's a lesbian or simply not happy with the choice available.

Clichés about lesbians are disgusting. They not only experience "classic" homophobia, like many gay men, but additional sexism of the worst kind. Lesbian women are considered either too butch, animalistic, or narcissistic, as philosopher Elizabeth Grosz wrote. Sadly, these attitudes don't seem to go extinct (Grosz & Probyn, 1995, p. 101).

In regard to literature, English Professor Valerie Rohy explains that lesbian sexuality is often either depicted as somehow insufficient, or as inacceptable, or even non-existent. Being a lesbian sadly is, she says, sometimes portrayed as "contagious, colonizing, and vampiric" (Rohy, 2000, p. 145).

All this is regrettable, and we have to continue fighting for an image of lesbian women that doesn't degrade them (and of course, not only because many of them are childfree).

Men don't face similar problems. They don't have to be fathers or grandpas; they don't need a pet either. Is it a cliché that lonesome cowboys—young or old—don't mind being alone? We all know men who stay in broken relationships only to have someone to yell at; this is not only a phenomenon among women. . . . Yet today's world remains a patriarchal one, which makes it much easier for men to adopt exactly the lifestyle they want and to defend it unconditionally.

This situation is especially unfair as Paul Dolan found out that among seniors, women are often less stressed out and more optimistic than their male peers. They volunteer more often and have bigger social networks. Dolan mentions the SDO: *Social Dominance Orientation*. This means supporting social hierarchies and more: "We are even willing to pay (literally, in cold hard cash) to punish people who we think have violated social convention" (Dolan 2019, p. xi).

The example of the cat lady clearly demonstrates how multiple discrimination works. You don't have to be a feminist to realize this. Being female guarantees you slut-shaming, body-shaming, and ageism—unless you die early. Thirty-nine seems to be a significant deadline, which I experienced personally. More than one journalist told me, when I was talking about my turning forty, that he was surprised to hear that; he saw a young woman, implying that forty is not young. Okay, maybe it isn't, compared to a student of eighteen, but why does a male journo who isn't that young himself talk to a woman he's about to interview in such a condescending way?

There was supposed to be a quirky compliment hidden somewhere, too. I heard that in his tone, but it didn't resonate with me. This seemed to surprise him. And (please!), how stupid (not to mention how utterly superficial) it is to fix youthfulness to a certain date/number. So, on the evening before my fortieth birthday, I was young or youngish, and on the morning after, I was suddenly old, overnight.

Walk of Shame (2014) is a movie that brilliantly shows how slut-shaming works. Meghan (Elizabeth Banks) is forty and actually a popular, successful newscaster. Yet when her car gets towed away (with her essential belongings inside), she quickly realizes what it's like to be a scantily dressed woman alone in Los Angeles. Ninety percent of the time, people think she's a prostitute, because she roams the streets in a short yellow dress and behaves slightly strangely from time to time.

Meghan meets men and women of different trades and classes who all agree in their negative judgment of her. A Black woman bus driver attacks her verbally and with pepper spray (well, she has no money and no bus ticket); on the very same bus an older lady tells her to be ashamed of herself. . . .

The employee of the impound lot is also especially nasty to Meghan when she tries to retrieve her car. Only two friends and her mother help her. This is monumentally depressing. Where is the kindness and (female) solidarity of strangers?

Misogyny is a horrible fact of life and if we participate in slut-shaming, it will never disappear. It's crucial that nobody fuel negative clichés about women, neither concerning their looks nor their private or professional behavior. This is not about refraining from necessary criticism (women, of course, make mistakes, just like men); it is about challenging stereotypes, which complicate women's lives unnecessarily. Female solidarity is important and should be encouraged from the earliest age on.

Spreading all such information remains taboo, which explains the outcry in Germany, Austria, and Switzerland when my book was published and the first interviews appeared. Dolan also confirms that it's difficult to speak *openly* about this topic. I argue that it's absolutely crucial not only to speak about it openly, but to promote the childfree lifestyle, to free it from all the negative labels attached to it so far.

Because *all* women are still chivvied into one direction: motherhood. Rebecca Solnit writes on the first page of her 2020 book *Recollections of My Nonexistence* about the question you always ask yourself: Are you good enough? If you're unlucky, your parents let you feel that the answer is no, although this way of educating kids has changed significantly. Nowadays, kids are ridiculously pampered. It must be bitter indeed to wake up in the real world to find out that you're not the center of everything.

If you're a man, you can go on living the way your mother brought you up; but for women, things are different. A whole industry, from make-up to cosmetic surgery, tells women every day that their appearance is somehow always lacking, no matter how hard they try. In addition, all other decisions you make are criticized by every Tom, Dick, and Harry—especially when it comes to one of life's most important: becoming a mother or not.

It can be enriching, observing the lifestyles of other people. Solnit writes how liberating the gay community in her neighborhood was for her. Liberation is contagious. . . . Yet so many people want to make motherhood compulsory instead of studying childfree women and the advantages they have. Solnit noticed that if gay people could openly and proudly reject a certain role, then she could do that too. In the penultimate chapter of her *Recollections*, she tells us about her witty comeback when pressured by the usual intrusive question about why she wasn't married and a mother: she lived in San

Francisco, a city that offers diverse interpretations of love, family, and kinship. The queer community taught her that friendship is a crucial element in our lives; that often friends are your "real" family; and that the conventions of pre-nups, consanguinity, procreation, and the like aren't all there is. Conservatives just aren't right.

While most parents would say that there's no discrimination against childfree/childless people, let me tell you—there is! I can't describe the extent of Othering I personally experienced, not to mention the stories I was told, books I read, or videos I watched that described what people without kids had to face. Discrimination can take many forms, as we all know, and if you are a victim, you can't escape. It doesn't have to be verbal or physical violence; condescending looks are often enough to make a victim feel absolutely inadequate and not welcome.

Susan Arndt, a German professor who writes about sexism, racism, and other prejudices, outlines several categories of people who usually face discrimination: she lists people of color, Jews, lesbians, transgender people, and others. But she fails to acknowledge that childfree people, especially women, are also victims of discrimination—in the workplace, politically, privately, and socially. This might have something to do with the fact that she's an overprivileged mother of four (Germany fawns over this type of mom).

In *Sexismus* (2020), she writes that motherhood is the best and most important and beautiful thing that has ever happened to her. This book is supposed to be about sexism, the work of a scholar, and so forth. Why oh why does she have to add this highly embarrassing eulogy about multiple motherhood, including dangerous downplaying of difficult pregnancies and deliveries? Things get even more cringeworthy when she talks about the medals German mothers received in the Third Reich: bronze for four children, silver for six, and eight or more got you gold. . . .

It's historically interesting that in the past there were various opportunities for women who wanted to stay childfree to fulfill their particular goals. In many monasteries throughout Europe, for example Töss in Switzerland, communities of well-educated nuns enjoyed each other's company—and that of the Lord's—as well as studying, working, and writing. Elsbeth Stagel, who lived in Töss (near Winterthur) at the beginning of the fourteenth century, wrote a book about the other nuns and their spiritual works and visions. Even back then, it was possible to find a way out, if your intention was to remain childfree. There are indeed hints in her book that some of the nuns had exactly this motivation, to reject life as a wife and mother. A few of them left this very life behind and joined the monastery later.

Regina Toepfer, a professor of Medieval Studies in Germany, published an impressive volume (in 2020) about parenting in the Middle Ages, in which she (who is childfree herself) shows in great detail how many different concepts of caring for children existed before the invention of the nuclear family much later. It wasn't unusual for noble families to send their child away to be educated elsewhere, for instance. Adoptions were also frequent and less problematic than they are nowadays. Spiritual mother- or fatherhood was quite common too. And, of course, fantastic "novels" like *Tristan* (which inspired Richard Wagner to compose his *Tristan und Isolde* in the nineteenth century) by the medieval poet Gottfried von Straßburg or *Parzival* by Wolfram von Eschenbach (Wagner also set this to music) have always featured heroes and heroines who are childfree. It's unthinkable that Tristan and Isolde, on a par with Romeo and Juliet, think or talk about children! Great romantic love excludes kids. . . .

Toepfer adds that degrading childfree/childless women—whether deliberately or not—is a prerequisite for the defense of the ideal of reproduction. Fertility problems and measures to solve them are traditionally attributed to the woman. Following Foucault, Toepfer argues that parenting is not a biological experience but a social construct. Infertility isn't a defect either, but rather socio-culturally, historically, and discursively determined. Since Luther's Reformation, nobody really challenges the notion that procreation is a good idea anymore.

Since most people have kids and therefore establish parenting as the norm, being childfree/childless turns you into the Other. In the Middle Ages, being without children was sometimes due to religious reasons. The nuns I mentioned before often thought they would serve the Lord better if they chose the path of chastity. On the other hand, many people tried everything to get rid of their infertility problems—just like today. And just like today, there's lots of superstition and making money out of desperate women. There's the pitiful capitalist reality of fertility tourism, exploiting women of poorer countries to help those of the West to become mothers eventually. (In fact, Renate Klein wrote a whole book from a radical feminist perspective on the problems arising from surrogacy). Surrogacy and prostitution are indeed similar: women who need money urgently sell their bodies (and souls—both institutions take a high psychological toll), and affluent people buy what shouldn't be on sale.

Elton John and his husband David Furnish, for example, are fathers to two young boys born this way. It's neither homophobia nor ageism that makes me criticize this couple; it's empathy with women who are in such a financial plight that they see no other option apart from egg donation, surrogacy, or prostitution. Patriarchy offers several possibilities for female bodies and body parts to be used and exploited.

There are always physical and psychological harms that the women in question suffer—all this for a few dollars. We have to help poor people in all countries so that they don't have to sell parts of themselves to rich Westerners. Of course, this isn't only a problem women have; I know a man from Iran who sold one of his kidneys because he was in desperate need of money.

Professor Arndt is not as progressive as the medieval nuns, she mentions her four kids again and again, which is a negative surprise in a book that is intended to come across as objective and scientific. However, she realizes correctly that Black women are often excluded when Western feminists talk about women "in general." White, European middle-class women: this is what traditional feminism is all about, Arndt argues. She also addresses the notion of compulsory heterosexuality, a term popularized by poet Adrienne Rich in her 1980 essay "Compulsory Heterosexuality and Lesbian Existence." These considerations are correct, but unfortunately, she doesn't see that it's the same for childfree/childless women. Janice Raymond's compulsory motherhood (1993) seems to be unknown to her. Rich and Arndt write that lesbian women are excluded from conventional femininity. But for an enormous number of people, women without kids aren't "real women" either.

Arndt doesn't downplay the sexist institution of prostitution, and she knows that violence is an inherent part. The degrading aspects of porn don't escape her either. However, her own behavior doesn't conform to these observations. She enjoys losing weight instead of fighting fat-shaming and endorsing body positivity. She explicitly talks about the male gaze she appreciates (that's really sad!). Drag star RuPaul's song (and catchphrase) comes to mind: "If you don't love yourself, how in the hell you gonna love somebody else?"

Fat-shaming is a huge problem in many countries. Beauty standards and personal preferences vary greatly in every region, but there's a strong tendency across societies to criticize plus-size people. In Europe and in the U.S., this trend has long been known and just won't disappear, although there are many campaigns against bullying in general and specifically against stigmatizing bigger people.

In England, class is an additional stigma—and not only there. British professor Paul Dolan writes of one (p. 144): "It's all those fat, lazy working-class folk that are crippling our beloved NHS." Of course, there's our beloved British humor in that, but it's a sad truth he expresses. People who aren't thin get all the blame for a failing health system; they are considered lazy—otherwise they wouldn't be fat, would they? *How about some work and exercising?*

Needless to say: women who are overweight are less accepted than men. There are men who never bring their plus-size girlfriend to gatherings because they fear harsh judgment and negative consequences.

If these women are childfree, they get additional vitriol: *Of course, someone like her didn't manage to attract any male's attention long enough to impregnate her.* Sadly, women also talk like this. A skinny colleague once said to me: "T. is single, isn't she? I mean, with those looks. . . . " This left me open-mouthed. Not only did it turn out that T. was a happily married woman with an adoring and adorable husband, but the colleague who'd talked about her in such a degrading way—a teacher who had studied, who educates teenagers—had *really* assumed that there couldn't be any man on Earth who'd fancy such an obese woman.

It's so important that childfree people raise their voice as a group and don't put up with being bullied anymore. If we denounce unfair treatment, then we become visible and encourage others to fight against injustice as well. Eventually, I hope, more and more people will doubt conventional morality concerning procreation. Finally, we could even change laws. There are not enough to speak out, but there are lots of co-perpetrators. . . .

New laws have been passed to protect women from harassment of all kinds, in the States, in Germany, and in many other countries. But where can you complain if an old gentleman living next door nods and says "You'd make a great mom"?

Many couples confirm the experts' findings. After my book release, lots of people wrote to me, telling me about their personal experiences. One such person was E.K., who complimented me on my manifesto, writing that it expressed verbally what his wife and he had been thinking for forty happy childfree years. He added that he'd had a vasectomy. Great man! He underlined that this choice was also a feminist one and that the intervention, which had taken place in day surgery, was only minimal.

Sterilization is worth talking about, as it's directly related to the topic at hand. A young woman contacted me and told me her story. F., nineteen, wanted to have her tubes tied. *Somehow*, she couldn't find a gynecologist willing to do that! Over and over, she had to hear condescending patriarchal remarks—also by the female physicians—concerning her young age and her fickleness. Lysann, another young woman, who was portrayed in a documentary and is active on YouTube, confirmed that it takes ages to find someone willing to do this. Interestingly enough, young women who express their desire to become mothers are usually encouraged. Are they less unstable? Or is it simply that their obedience, their docility, and their willing fulfillment of cultural norms gets them all this adulation for a purely biological process?

Feminists around the globe agree: such discrimination is always about systemic patriarchal ideals and norms and sexism at its base level. The "reasons" why physicians denied women tubal ligation were collected and mostly fell into concerns about the woman's age, their not being married, and their childfree state (Chan & Westoff 2010).

To sum it up: these women might regret their choice later in life. This implies that the medical establishment doesn't trust women to make good choices for themselves. This is outrageous! Especially as no one is telling aspiring mothers that they might regret their children (which is statistically more likely).

3.2 Abortion

Abortion (a crucial feminist issue) is under sustained attack around the globe. Infertility, on the other hand, is considered a horrible fate, much more of a pain than any real disease. Physicians cash in on some couples' desperation by providing several services to remedy this terrible disadvantage. Is this the right way to go about it?

The great anti-natalist philosopher David Benatar, who will be presented in detail in Chapter 4, argues that "it is wrong to help somebody inflict the harm of bringing somebody into existence" (Benatar 2007, p. 128).

Infertility treatments are expensive and often dangerous or disagreeable for the female body—yet many women willingly undergo them. Wouldn't it be a much better idea to focus on women's minds, to empower them deeply by showing them what to do with their lives, instead of helping them with a project that will have lots of negative effects anyway?

Not so in our current times. In fact, we can't help noticing a severe backlash. Giving birth has been seen as the norm forever. If you don't reproduce, you have at least to be unhappy about it. Being childless gets you people's pity; but being childfree is a guarantee of being bullied.

In the Middle Ages, childlessness was a stigma that could indeed ruin your life. For instance, a noble lady's main function was to provide an heir to the estate or the throne. Being fruitful and multiplying was taken seriously by most of the population back then—and more and more do this as well in the year 2022—which is not only part of the backlash we're describing, but an ecological disaster.

More and more people also discriminate against childfree people, first and foremost female ones. People with children are bombarded with various pieces of advice, whether medical, religious, or social, because they at least try to fulfill societal norms. *But those childfree guys—aren't they just crazy?*

No wonder that research concerning possible reasons for infertility or impotence has always been prominent—and profitable. You can never be sure that the concoctions the medical establishment (now and in the past) has come up with will work—but at least you have to try them. Now and then, there are court cases because of the inability to reproduce. There are medieval songs and paintings praising huge families and pitying couples with no kids. In the Middle Ages, couples with children were glorified, whereas those who are childfree are vilified. It's the same today.

Some cultural norms have persisted. Gender Studies and Dis/Ability Studies don't help much when it comes to the core question: reproduction. Some of the medieval nuns could be seen as childfree pioneers, however. They opted out of parenthood, living a life of chastity in a monastery, praying, writing, etc.

Nevertheless, infertility has never been seen as a blessing, which is what I would like people to reconsider. Who says that fertility is more valuable than infertility? Why is there still some kind of hierarchy that puts the fertile above the others? Let's challenge that instead of being reminded of the Middle Ages all the time!

There are also similarities to cosmetic surgery. Why do people inflict bodily harm on themselves in order to fulfill norms that aren't progressive at all when they could have therapy to boost their low self-esteem? But no, they want to try everything to produce a first-world baby of their own, regardless of full orphanages.

Caitlin Moran writes that said first-world babies eat our planet like termites and that motherhood didn't offer her one lesson that couldn't have been learned elsewhere. In her book *How to Be a Woman*, she also admits that she would gladly have shot the world's last panda (!) if that had meant that her baby would have cried sixty seconds less. . . . This is meant as a joke, but nonetheless outrageous.

Leslie Kern admits that her political activism declined significantly after she gave birth. Why is that? Because babies aren't safe during a demonstration or strike? Or because the woman's mentality changes, focusing on the child's needs? She doesn't know either. Kern also admits that many crimes against women happen in the home. Their kids' fathers are the ones to blame—yet media portrayals show us the picture of the home as a safe place for every woman and mother, unlike dangerous streets, where potential assaults lurk around every corner. If the newspaper or TV channel is right-wing, it usually blames foreign men, depicting them as the only threat to native women. Kern gets this right, as well as the fact that danger comes more often from police officers being sexist and not really helping women, and not your average refugee roaming the streets, who's really having other problems. And the streets aren't that dangerous; often it's public transport, even if you don't live in India. (Everyone remembers the horrible rape of a young woman in Delhi by several men on a bus in 2012.)

Stockholm, Sweden, and Geneva, Switzerland, banned sexist commercials in public spaces to make them safer for women, because the authorities realized that stereotypes of this kind worsen the way men treat real women.

It's biology that parents care for their offspring. But why do they do it in such a way that really disgusts people who choose a different lifestyle? Having your priorities straight is one thing; complete recklessness another.

At least Moran recognizes that "[w]e need more women who are allowed to prove their worth as people, rather than being assessed merely for their potential to create new people" (p. 45).

Back to reproductive medicine. Reproduction is considered a human right. Yet, there are already almost eight billion people on this planet. But you can't tell people not to have kids, can you? Well, John Stuart Mill could. The nineteenth-century utilitarian was an advocate of restricting the birth rate. The philosopher was also known as a feminist who worked closely with his wife Harriet to promote women's liberation in England. One of their core issues was contraception. And how advanced they were!

Mill wasn't the only one who was relatively progressive. The French painter Pierre-Auguste Renoir produced many works depicting women reading. Likewise, Henri de Toulouse-Lautrec. The British writer Isaac D'Israeli (father of British prime minister Benjamin Disraeli) explicitly stated that women have more interests than procreation and superficialities.

Mill's pet project is still highly relevant today, with 214 million women and girls who want contraception but do not currently have access to it, and 99 million unplanned pregnancies a year.

Feminism, and especially radical feminism, has always fought for women's reproductive rights. How can you lead a self-determined life if patriarchy consistently interferes with *your* decisions concerning *your* body? Bodily autonomy is a human right and it's absolutely ludicrous that so-called pro-lifers keep trying to infringe women's rights in the name of the unborn. It's not about them. It's about patriarchal control over women's bodies and *lives*.

If women abort, it's usually not a caprice. It's something nobody does because they are whimsical. They are in distress; they think about their decision—being under high pressure because of the short period of time they are allowed; and they finally make this decision, which should be supported unconditionally. They don't kill a person; they get rid of a clump of cells!

It's just not fair because, as Benatar notes, "a legal pro-choice position does not require a pro-lifer to have an abortion—it allows a choice—a legal pro-life position does prevent a pro-choicer from having an abortion" (p. 224).

"Pro-lifers" are mostly people who are not only anti-feminist, but also racist, homophobic, and nationalistic. This is fairly typical because fascistic regimes *always* rely on loads of new native babies. If "your own" numbers are up, you have the best excuse to keep "the others" out—those evil immigrants who only take your jobs, your money, and your women. . . . (This issue is enlarged upon in Chapter 3.) Women should really think twice if they want to help such people fulfill their horrible white supremacist goals.

What we need is more support of women and girls who do not want to contribute to overpopulation, fascism, environmental destruction, and anti-feminism. This entails a clear pro-choice policy and free birth control for everyone. Some cities already hand out condoms for free, but we need much more than that. Every person seeking sterilization should have our full support—not the opposite.

Of course, we also need more research concerning possible methods of contraception for men. It's a pity that in 2022, the vast majority of women are still responsible for this issue. Men are fertile thirty days a month, women for only very few days—yet they take on this task, often risking several side effects, especially related to hormonal contraceptives.

Women use pills and patches, injections and implants, rings and cups and sponges. It's high time that men actively do something. Yes, condoms are a great invention. You just have to buy and wear them.

Still, female tubal ligation is a much more popular contraception method, if you look at UN statistics.

There might be some hope, though: Sujoy Guha, seventy-eight years old, is an Indian biomedical engineer and has come up with a syringe that can be shot into the male tubes. His drug is called Risug (reversible inhibition of sperm under guidance) and is basically a viscous gel that inactivates the sperm (Chattopadhay 2012). It could be effective for thirteen years, his research team says. It's also non-hormonal, which means no harmful side effects like those that women risk when they're on the pill.

3.3 Sex Life

Recalling Johnson's results about the happiness of childfree couples, it is sad to see daily proof of the reverse. Many women have told me their heartbreaking stories of failed marriages—not in spite of the fact that they are mothers, but *because* of it!

So-called traditional models are especially dangerous for women. One woman, V., 51, informed me that the father of her three kids had abandoned her for another woman, leaving her alone with no income and a shitload of chores. It sounds like a cliché, yet everyone knows lots of women who have suffered similarly. And is it really a consolation that the kids stay with you, while he amuses himself with the new girl? Everyone hopes that this will happen to other women, but looking at divorce rates, to think so is naive.

Leslie Ashburn-Nardo, who has been conducting research in this field for forty years, arrives at the same conclusions. As she wrote in the magazine *Demography* in 2015, a newborn's effect on a couple is harder than divorce, unemployment, or even the death of your partner! She has conducted many studies concerning this topic, and they all confirm children have a negative impact on relationships. Yet many of Ashburn-Nardo's fellow Americans react morally outraged to childfree people.

In Great Britain, an Open University study with more than 5,000 participants verifies this: childfree couples are happier than parents (Open University 2013). That seems self-evident. Your relationship is about you and your partner; you feel appreciated and content. This is contrary to what parents have to go through: endless organizing, projects revolving around the kids, education quarrels, and so on.

Nevertheless, it becomes more and more of an imperative to procreate, which also means that your freedom of choice is about to dwindle. The world becomes more and more hostile for non-breeders.

In 1971, Ellen Peck's book *The Baby Trap* was published. She revealed reasons that prompted couples to have a child that aren't as glorious as many parents want us to believe. The desire to conform featured prominently, so did boredom (!), as well as the mini-me alarm. For some, it seems to be a real turn-on to hear sentences like "Oh, I love your beautiful eyes, let's make a baby that also has these eyes!" I already mentioned that I don't share this opinion—quite the contrary.

Many first-hand stories of parents emphasize that their erstwhile sex life was going downhill from the second they decided to "try for a baby." No wonder! This project seems to involve strange procedures: you must have sex at five p.m. sharp, in a certain position of course. It's also important to eat special food, to abstain from substances you'd normally enjoy, and to listen to Mozart (even before conceiving).

Afterward, you have to make sure that every measure is taken to guarantee the success of your biological experiment. The desperation of couples who "fail" is well-known. But the "lucky" ones, who are proud parents nine months, later complain about their love life if you question them privately.

One example is S., aged 33. She told me confidentially (naturally, most usually don't admit it publicly—who would?) that she and her husband didn't have a real sex life anymore. Everything in their life was always about J., their little daughter. Either J. slept in the bed with them (well . . .) or S. was too tired and exhausted from running after her child the whole day. She revealed that she wasn't really happy about this state of things but was somehow unable to do anything about it. She added that her priorities centered on her daughter, which is completely understandable, but still—S. is a lovely young woman and it's sad to know that she has virtually no sex life anymore.

Some parents manage to get away on a romantic weekend from time to time. Yet the question remains: Does that really make up for all those nights when you tried to sneak in five minutes but were crudely separated by a newborn wailing in the next room?

It seems to be mostly mothers who get up at night when their children have health problems or nightmares, or any other issues. While there's a certain logic for mothers doing this when they're breastfeeding, it's less comprehensible that they still do it when the children are at elementary school. Maybe it has become a habit.

The kids seem to frequently boast about things like this! One boy, 12, told a highly amusing story (in his opinion) about his mom, who had to get up in the middle of the night when the friend who stayed over had vomited in his room.

Whole novels have been written on the phenomenon of parents who desperately try to have a pleasant evening without interruption. This challenge is not to be underestimated, because a happy sex life is crucial for your mental and physical health. (We're not talking about singles, asexual people, or people opting for different lifestyles altogether; this is about couples trying to make their relationship work, although it is possible to be happy and healthy if you both choose not to have sex.)

So, one answer to one of my initial questions—Do childfree people have better sex?—is that *at least they usually still have* sex! To open the nursery is to close the bedroom.

Childfree people also don't have to organize this event weeks before, something that's likely to kill any romantic feelings, when you have to be in the mood that very evening because you know that if you aren't, you'll have to wait ages till a similar situation occurs.

I'd go even further. One mother talked about her self-esteem on the radio, for everyone to listen to. Well, she actually talked about a shopping spree with her young daughter. It was supposed to be funny, but it was actually sad, because the woman described her figure, which she obviously found wanting, and immediately she justified herself: it wasn't her "duty" to look good anymore, she was a mother! She went into a changing cubicle, taking her child with her. Undressing, she was even more unhappy and her daughter confirmed her opinion: "Not beautiful, mommy!"

Well, children and fools tell the truth, the mother consoled herself. This struck me as wrong on so many levels. Why on Earth was it this mother's "duty" before she gave birth to please anyone but herself? Why did she accept criticism from a little child? And why had her small daughter already internalized not only how to put other women down (even your own mother!), but also questionable beauty standards?

This radio show was further proof that children aren't good for your self-esteem, as several studies have found. So, who do you prefer to have sex with? A person with low or high self-esteem? I think it's way more delightful with a person you're on a par with. A person who is an interesting conversation partner, for starters. A man or woman who has a full life with fascinating stories to tell, with empathy toward you—and not with one primary concern always on their mind.

I can't imagine having sex with someone on whose clothes there are still remnants of baby vomit, who talks about children's nutrition and excretions, and so forth. Are mommies and daddies really still sexy? I personally don't think so. And, as nature itself is sometimes misogynistic, women's bodies always suffer from pregnancy and childbirth. There'll always be marks on them. Of course, men who turned those poor ladies into mothers have to put up with all that (and there are plenty of pretentious fathers who aren't prepared to do so!), but childfree people usually prefer the minds, bodies, and souls of similar people and it's their right: nothing presumptuous there.

Of course, organizing a family is hard work (*a mother's work is never done* and all that), but one can easily imagine that it also affects the spark that once existed between the couple. Arguments about education or money (rather less frequent among childfree couples) often add to the anti-romanticism ruling households with children.

You can't be *really* spontaneous, either, if you have a kid. You may have seen a "funny" video about young parents: the woman hectically shaves, cuts herself, smears lipstick on her face, and tells her hubby that it's now or never. Little Archie has just gone to sleep. Hubby rises to the occasion (despite the less-than-romantic invitation), also runs to the bathroom, freshens up, and joins his woman in bed. Just as they begin to kiss desperately, Archie starts crying. They manage to get him quiet again and want to take up where they left off. But as they are in such a hurry, the woman slips on a carpet and falls, and the man hurts himself when he tries to help her.

One could cry watching this! Of course, the video is exaggerated, but seemingly not that much. Who'd want to live like that? It kills any lust that might have remained if you became parents.

Another reason why childfree people usually have better sex is that there are many places that are always available for a quickie—whenever you feel like it (and not only when the kid is asleep or out of the way). People without children mostly have no toys cluttering floors, tables, and other surfaces. They tend to live in lovely apartments or houses and not crammed in with their offspring and their paraphernalia. They also have cars that don't resemble a trash heap or a toy store. If childfree people own a car (some are immensely environmentally conscious in this respect), it's usually a cool one, maybe a double-seater, seldom an SUV that looks horrible and kills the planet.

Apart from that, your imagination isn't used up by planning children's birthday parties, and your time and energy aren't consumed by hurrying through a tight schedule that leaves you exhausted at the end of the day. Childfree people have the leisure to focus on their partner and their feelings and desires, which improves each relationship almost automatically. Being each other's No. 1 is one of the reasons childfree couples give when asked about their decision to remain childfree.

Sleep is another crucial parameter. If you're tired all the time, your sex life suffers. In a study published in the journal *Sleep* in January 2019, researchers from the University of Warwick, West Virginia University, and the German Institute for Economic Research found that sleep duration and satisfaction dropped significantly for parents at childbirth and reached rock bottom three months later (Pearson 2019). Breastfeeding mothers are especially affected (no surprise there). According to the study, age, income, or marital status didn't have any effect. The most important result of the study was that it takes six whole years until the parents' sleep patterns start to resemble what they were before they had a child! Who wants that?

It's not surprising that women are more concerned by this problem than men because of the distribution of care work. Also, after those fatal six years, as I mentioned earlier, it's usually the mother who gets up in the middle of the night when a child has a nightmare or vomits.

As the childfree also have enough time and money to enjoy their lives, they are usually well-learned and more active in their passions. This not only heightens their sex appeal, but also makes them more sensitive as well as open and imaginative partners too. If you focus *totally* on the beloved person in bed with you (or wherever you happen to find yourself . . .) and not on your genes or the act of reproduction, you reach a level of exclusive, intense intimacy unknown to those who are keen on producing a mini-me and often consider their partner as means to an end.

The best partners within the group of childfree men are feminists. They know a lot about the female body, and what's more important, they respect it and treat it accordingly. They want to make their women happy, unlike those macho guys who aren't really interested in their partners' pleasure.

Feminists know there is such a thing as a nipple orgasm, and they'll make an effort to achieve it. They also know the G-spot or the clitourethrovaginal (CUV) complex, and how to stimulate both. They also know there are still women who fake an orgasm—in 2022, and two years after the death of Shere Hite, who'd again and again criticized this phenomenon in her *Reports* in the 1970s, 80s, and 90s.

Okay, *Men's Health* (not really a feminist magazine) sometimes tries to encourage men to be sensitive lovers. But it's a question of attitude. If you scanned the article about nipple orgasm because of the pictures of breasts going with it, this is different from a feminist reading it in order to learn more about how the female body works and what he can do to satisfy his partner.

Feminists don't watch porn, so they won't ask their partners to shave or behave like one of the actresses in those videos. Anal waxing and/or bleaching or even operations won't be required. Sadly, some girls and women who had nose or boob jobs are role models for teenagers who want to be like them, because they believe they'll be successful and popular, too, when they modify their natural beauty in this way. . . . What these young ladies don't get is that you attract a type of man with questionable standards. He's hardly likely to be a feminist who makes efforts to gratify his girlfriend.

It's also depressing when female physicians write books about breasts that include whole chapters on how to keep your cleavage attractive for the male gaze—all your life! Carmen Jochem, a doctor and mother of three, published a fairly successful book about this topic in 2020, although she mainly talked about breastfeeding and keeping one's décolleté pretty. There were at least some hints on how to avoid cancer.

Feminists also know more about female psychology. They don't pamper women unconditionally, but they understand if you're a bit more aggressive or depressed before starting your period. They ask themselves if the menstruating woman likes sex during these days or not, and not (only) if they want it. Feminists don't behave obnoxiously only because there's a frightening number of women who fancy bad boys.

Criteria like age, figure, income, and other superficial aspects aren't that important in a healthy relationship, I argue. For a psychically and physically fulfilling relationship, there are different criteria. Does the guy in question respect every woman? How does he treat (for instance) older women, waitresses, etc.? Narcissists without empathy will betray themselves soon and aren't worth spending time with. They want and need dependent, submissive women they can treat like dolls or pets.

Many childfree couples are fed up with our child-obsessed society. To celebrate their lifestyle, they have events such as vasectomy parties. Nothing wrong with that, you'd think, and yet they get all the hatred annoyed breeders have obviously pent up within them—and that's a lot! You'd imagine that educating children would take up all your time and energy, but the anti-socials among the breeders still have lots of both to direct insults and hate speech toward innocent childfree people. There seems to be a direct correlation: If they don't educate their kids properly, they have more time to insult the childfree online. . . .

These "parents" also don't refrain from criminal words and actions; it's incredible that such people have children! Maybe they're just unhappy because they ruined their lives (and not only their sex lives). But is this the childfree community's fault? Sometimes, you can't shake off the impression that it's parents who aren't able to accomplish much else in their lives who behave in such an aggressive way. Passing on one's genes is easier than earning five dollars, an old German proverb tells us. Well, that's certainly true.

Wes Siler, a 38-year-old who writes *Indefinitely Wild*, a lifestyle column (Siler 2019), talked about how his vasectomy procedure "ended up being quicker and less invasive than most dental appointments. I took off my pants, laid on a bed, received a local anesthetic, chatted with the doctor while he made a few incisions, then got a ride home. Once the anesthetic wore off, it felt like someone had kicked me in the balls pretty good, a feeling that dissipated over the next seven days. I took a Valium before the surgery and a few handfuls of ibuprofen afterward but otherwise didn't need painkillers or even an ice pack. The worst part was taking a week off from the gym; I'd been making good progress.It might not be enough to save the polar bear, and it might not prevent the next [California] Camp Fire [wildfire], but this is the absolute biggest difference we can make."

What a brilliant person! We need more like him. Siler briefly outlines how much he can save by not having any kids, and how every single child would feed the cycle of consumption, however "green" he might raise them. Correct. I know virtually no students who haven't had several smartphones in their short lives. Yes, wearing earphones as a young girl might help you to avoid being molested in the streets all the time—we managed with our Walkman or Discman. But does every ten-year-old need the latest smartphone? How do people in Asian or African countries cope, where street life may be more dangerous than in the West?

This is also true for Nicolas, who lives in Berlin and wrote to me on Facebook that my activism had finally helped him make the decision to have a vasectomy as well.

Reproduction seems to hold a special appeal for conservatives. They might pursue a career, but it's seldom a real vocation, and their main goal is to earn a lot. Property and material possessions are of great value for these people (and it all comes together: you need to accumulate wealth, the kids want a considerable financial inheritance and not only a dying planet. . .). Usually, they vote accordingly. They are church-goers, often have several subscriptions to various dull magazines, and plan their vacations months or even years in advance. They try to be role models for their children, at least officially (hence the nasty term *sanctimommy*), but unfortunately, there's lots of hypocrisy in their behavior. They'll be absolutely bourgeois, in their personal appearance and taste: they are never car-free; they like the police, the army, and our capitalist system in general; and their main concern is the opinion of other mediocre people. Fulfilling their full potential as a person is less important than "having success" as others would define it. A flashy car, a neat house, a great career, the "right" partner, two kids—that's about it. Is that really an individual dream, a dream worth sacrificing everything for?

But isn't it a bit sad when one's dream is such a conformist vision, a path trodden by almost everyone else now and before? I think as human beings in the twenty-first century, we should aim higher—especially, as major system changes are necessary—if the world is supposed to persist, ideally, as a better world, one without exploitation of any kind.

Those with children often accuse the childfree of moralizing. If you come out as a vegetarian who doesn't fly and has no kids, something must be wrong with you. *Why would someone voluntarily be such a killjoy for themselves and others*, they usually imply. Well, here's news. . . . There are *some* joys and pleasures I would *never* abstain from. I'm talking about food, of course.

If you board a plane, the environment suffers. But if you have sex for mutual fulfillment, to celebrate your happiness with a person you absolutely adore—then not only suffering can be avoided completely, but total bliss can be the result.

As a woman—but also as a man—contraception isn't an issue if you have a same-sex partner. It's often only social convention that makes women shut both eyes if they find an interesting woman appealing to them in every respect. I recommend opening up to all sexes and genders, because doing so will enrich you personally. The barriers to that experience were artificially constructed anyway, and it's much more natural to feel attracted to great personalities, regardless of their gender.

Rita Mae Brown did a lot for me in this respect, although I never saw the sense of limiting myself concerning my range of possible partners. Why exclude fifty percent only because they are female, too? This is just crazy! Many scholars have argued that heteronormativity is socially constructed—and not the natural order of things, as conservatives want us to believe. Lots of people are actually bisexual and either repress it in order to conform, or don't admit it openly.

Likewise with female masturbation. While boys are mostly encouraged to masturbate and everyone tacitly accepts their use of pornography, it's not always okay for girls. It's not only puritan parents who imply, or state directly, that masturbation is dirty or something to be ashamed of. Girls are reminded of the image of the saint, the woman without sexuality, who is pure and chaste and completely unsoiled, even though a fraction of religious people only have sex after marriage and in order to procreate. It's vital for modern girls and women to know themselves, and to find out everything they can about their own personal sexual needs and longings— because they may well realize that a man is not the only possible answer to their ardent questions.

3.4 Polyamory

Polyamory is another lifestyle conservatives hate—and, of course, it's women much more than men who are criticized when they come out. Why is that? "Cultural conditioning, unruly emotions, peer pressure, or social censure," writes the late American clinical psychologist Deborah Anapol, an expert in this field (Anapol 2012). Unfortunately, she died in 2015, after decades of activism. Anapol is considered a founder of the polyamory movement, which started in the 1980s. Like other activists who challenge mainstream notions, Anapol received lots of negative comments.

What has polyamory to do with feminism or childfree living? It's the traditional nuclear family which keeps women down!

Monogamy isn't for everyone. Just like some men, some women are also plainly unhappy when they have to curb their longings. It's high time we said goodbye to the notion that living with one partner all your life (like some birds do) is either morally superior or the best option for every human creature.

Not everyone lives in a big city where it's cool to cultivate your life—and love style the way you want it. We need visible role models. In Season Eight of *RuPaul's Drag Race*, we meet a Britney Spears impersonator by the name of Derrick Barry. Barry has two boyfriends, and they've formed a happy throuple for years. This is great! Obviously, many people might think a throuple is a gay thing, "normal straight" people wouldn't do that, but this is just wrong.

Of course, much can be said against *Drag Race* from a feminist point of view, the most significant being that it perpetuates or even heightens stereotypes. The episodes often show performers who call each other bitch incessantly, caring only about their clothes and make-up or about servicing men. Nevertheless, *Drag Race* does a lot for gay rights, taking a stand against homophobia by delivering such great entertainment that skeptics can be won over.

There's certainly aesthetic pleasure in watching, for example, Violet Chachki or Miss Fame. Celebrating beauty should be open to all genders and it's definitely not anti-feminist to find delight in looking at a gorgeous face, whether it's female, male, or something in-between. If you don't objectify or degrade the person you're watching, all should be okay.

I've heard of throuples/poly constellations consisting of two women and a man; or two men and one woman; or more people. It all depends on whom you fall in love with. It's a myth that polyamory is indecisive heterosexual men forcing two women to pretend to like his ménage à trois. Real polyamory involves the consent of everyone participating.

In his book *Insatiable Wives*, David Ley writes that women who don't adhere to monogamy have great communication skills. One of his clients told him he could also relax most when being around close friends or lovers—plural. Having more than one partner made him happy, which also had positive effects on his other relationships, his own health, and state of mind (Ley 2012).

Polyamory is for people who are open and honest, who want to grow, who need freedom, and who think profoundly about topics like loyalty, romanticism, and philosophical ideals. Free spirits who don't have problems with being judged by mainstream people. These progressive personalities often are better educated and more intelligent in general, aren't religious, and often identify as bisexual. The women especially—what a surprise!—are sometimes discriminated against, but they have been playing significant roles from the beginning of the polyamory movement heretofore. More than half of them are bisexual (cf. Anapol, Chapter 2).

Loving relationships can go in so many possible directions: Why does it have to be one man and one woman? Monogamy is compulsory, even more so than heterosexuality. From childhood on, we are fed stories and cultural constructions that claim many people lie, but monogamy is nevertheless the ideal we should all aspire to. We're educated to accept controlling and possessive mentalities not as negative, but completely normal. Does it have to be this way?

It's true that it's not particularly easy to say goodbye to exclusiveness, especially for very proud people, but one gets used to the new situation quickly—and not only because the plethora of advantages convinces everyone in the end. Some poly arrangements imitate bourgeois families, including establishing protocols where every single right or task is written down. These are the exceptions, though. Usually, polyamory is all about authenticity and autonomy.

Honesty and respect are more important than sexual exclusivity. Nonetheless, it's a challenge to stop concealing things; it's the way most of us were socialized.

Plenty of books describe the role of hormones in adult human mating rites, but one should be careful. Biology has often been misused to enforce the alleged superiority of men; for instance, in suggesting that it was nature itself that led women toward motherhood and monogamy, whereas men, as former hunters, were destined to woo every female crossing their path.

The French philosopher Charles Fourier (1772–1837) was convinced every person had some capacity to love more than one partner—on a scale of zero to ten, with most of us somewhere in between. Fourier also fought for gay rights and sexual freedom. His ideas weren't about motivating those who were on zero or one to try multiple partners; they were rather about showing women who were near ten that nothing was wrong with them, and that how they behaved was normal. Still nowadays, many women feel ashamed when they listen to themselves instead of letting patriarchy rule their lives. Emma Goldman is an interesting voice here, too. The feminist anarchist crusaded for contraception and free love in times when women weren't allowed to vote.

Anapol asks why, many decades later, women, "who are generally less likely than men to reach orgasm through intercourse or to reach orgasm at all if their lover is unskilled, are reputed to be more likely to remain attached, while their male partners seek variety" (Anapol 2012, ch. 1).

She also writes that seventy percent of all couples have experience with affairs. Fantasies involving non-monogamous activities should be talked about, Anapol reckons. Often one could avoid a divorce if both partners were open to communicating desires they deemed prohibited.

In 2007, Bavarian conservative politician Gabriele Pauli suggested that a marriage should lapse every seven years and vows renewed only if the marriage was still what it was supposed to be. She was widely ridiculed throughout Germany, although we know that "breaking free from the narrative of monogamy will reduce the suffering of women most of all," as Paul Dolan writes (2019, p. 86). He has a convincing reason: women lose interest in sex earlier in long-term relationships. Oscar Wilde shocked Britain and the world when, in *The Picture of Dorian Gray*, his character Lord Henry says that "the only way to get rid of a temptation is to yield to it." A new allurement is a new allurement, period. It's not necessarily that one is bored by known allurements, but if the occasion is there. . . .

Dolan also lists money, power, and the big city, where many attractions present themselves around every corner. And yet in the U.S., eighty-four percent of people find affairs unacceptable; in Great Britain it's seventy-six. Europe is more relaxed in this respect, especially in the East. In Muslim countries, the acceptance rate is very low (ibid., p. 81).

Dolan has yet more interesting information. Talking about the frequency of sexual encounters between partners, he found that men exaggerated while women played things down. This is not surprising, as women with lots of partners must endure slut-shaming. Men with many partners, on the other hand, are admired by their peers and popular with women. When Dolan's team mentioned a lie detector in their survey (ibid., p. 82), the statements between men and women suddenly became quite similar. Dolan writes: "optimal marital satisfaction [is] associated with sex once a week, and lower satisfaction with less and more frequent sex than this (p. 83)."

Polyamory is an option worth considering, when you are happy in a relationship but meet someone new whom you surprisingly fall in love with. Almost everyone would be in a horrible dilemma, wondering whom to give up, making more than one person unhappy. But if everyone makes an effort, it's possible to create something new without destroying something you already hold dear.

A big advantage is that the expectations you had can be divided, thus making life easier for all participants. It's unrealistic that one person can fulfill every need and wish of their partner, whether we talk about favorite vacation destinations, food, sports, what to watch together, and so on.

Why not just be friends with people we share one particular passion with? Fair enough. But why not share an additional passion if the spark is there and if all people concerned consent? It's hypocritical to say there are no interesting third or fourth people around, so why not acknowledge it and enrich the eroticism instead of accepting its death sooner or later, which is unfortunately a problem in many monogamous relationships.

Accepting a third person is a great sign of the strength and stability of an existing relationship, in my opinion. It's also a sign of unconditional love. Does one fall out of love only because our partner meets another attractive person? Anapol and other professionals dealing with polyamory confirm that this usually only ruins relationships that hadn't been working anyway; in all other cases, it had no effect or was even stabilizing.

It's of course wrong to suffer silently and hope that a dead marriage or a wish to be with someone else is just a phase. Communicating one's feelings is key and complete honesty helps a lot. Some women have said they weren't in favor of polyamory at first, but discovered that it gave them a completely new way of looking at the world. Some met other men who were then added. Often, the new energy had invigorating effects on sex with the partner they'd had for years.

Self-confidence is also a characteristic of people who love more than one person. Security, control, and predictability make some stay monogamous, even if they secretly want a different life. But courage, creativity, and flexibility can change any problem into a challenge.

Polyamory can be a problem when partners live in different cities. Organizing and planning is of course essential. But people who opt for polyamory are usually strong, creative, independent, and extroverted, anyway. More important than logistic complications are emotional intricacies, which can arise if/when one partner feels neglected. Even open, tolerant people sometimes feel jealousy. Deborah Anapol's book *Compersion: Meditations on Using Jealousy as a Path to Unconditional Love* (2005) lists helpful ideas on how to cope with this problem. Simple strategies like breathing exercises can be a start.

The French writer Roland Barthes wonders in 1977: "et si je me forçais à n'être plus jaloux, par honte de l'être? C'est laid, c'est bourgeois, la jalousie [. . .] Comme jaloux, je souffre quatre fois: parce que je suis jaloux, parce que je me reproche de l'être, parce que je crains que ma jalousie ne blesse l'autre, parce que je me laisse assujettir à une banalité: je souffre d'être exclu, d'être agressif, d'être fou et d'être commun." ("What if I forced myself not to be jealous, out of shame. Jealousy is ugly, bourgeois [. . .]. Being jealous, I suffer four times over: because I'm jealous; because I reproach myself for being jealous; because I fear my jealousy will hurt the other person; and because I allow myself to be subjected to banality. I suffer from being excluded, from being aggressive, from being crazy, and from being common.")

He's right, of course, jealousy is bourgeois, yet there is almost nobody who hasn't experienced this feeling at least once in their life. For some it's harder to realize that love does multiply, that if my partner loves another person, too, this doesn't mean his love for me has diminished. There are many prejudices concerning jealousy: to be jealous doesn't mean you have lower self-esteem; women don't always judge other women's looks; or men other guys' income or status. Talking about jealousy—with those concerned and/or other friends, maybe a therapist—helps most people. If you meet the "new person," you usually find out quickly why your partner feels so attracted to them.

Writers such as Shakespeare and composers such as Giuseppe Verdi or Gioachino Rossini in their respective versions of Othello show us how lethal jealousy can become, for at least two people involved. The protagonist is successful and has a loving wife, but he kills her in the end, because he believes Iago's rumors about her conduct. Othello may only be a drama or an opera (*Otello*), but the thousands of women killed every year by a jealous husband or boyfriend shine a different light on things.

There is almost no Italian opera that doesn't feature jealousy—it's everything that Verdi wrote! Vincenzo Bellini's *Norma* explores the feelings of a jealous woman, the eponymous priestess, whose ex (also the father of her two kids) is now in a relationship with Adalgisa, another priestess. Psychologically brilliant, Bellini writes music for the orchestra that reflects Norma's feelings, so we have double impact: not only does the text show the audience her inner self, but the accompaniment reflects it. You don't need operas or novels or plays, though, to realize that jealousy can be a negative emotion that doesn't help anyone. Sometimes, jealousy and envy aren't differentiated sufficiently.

Some people only open their relationship on one side. (Well, whatever makes them happy.) Others can accept one more person, but no more. I consider agreements about what's allowed with a new sexual partner to be bourgeois. Genuine polyamory wouldn't impose any restrictions.

I'm reminded of White House intern Monica Lewinsky, whose affair with President Bill Clinton led to the question of whether oral sex was actually sex. . . . I'm also thinking of the case of Anne Sinclair and her violent former husband, the French finance minister Dominique Strauss-Kahn. Strauss-Kahn had lots of sexual encounters, even forced ones, including with prostitutes. He was even accused by a chambermaid of sexual assault in New York State in 2011. What Strauss-Kahn did is definitely not polyamory; it's just plain cruelty. It's hard to fathom why Myriam L'Aouffir, twenty years his junior, married this man in 2017.

The world is full of men who commit honor killings. Women all over the world are stalked, threatened, and often murdered by men they once loved, who are often the fathers of their children. Following feminist writers such as Janice Raymond, Catharine MacKinnon, or Melissa Farley, we must fight everything that creates special problems for women alone. Freedom for a woman can only mean she doesn't have to be submissive in order to be popular, or a mother in order to be respected by the world. No woman should be forced to sell her body or parts of it out of sheer desperation and a lack of alternatives.

Sheila Jeffreys, 72, tells us in her autobiography *Trigger Warning* (2020) how difficult it can be to combat myths such as those of the happy sex worker. She considers reproduction detrimental to female progress and is, of course, childfree herself. As in my case, she says that haters, stalkers, and other criminals, who can't read and write properly and who have never seen, touched, or opened any of her books, compose horrible Amazon reviews and belittle and demean her.

Those who combat white men's privileges have to pay the price. Whenever it's possible, such women are also ignored and ridiculed.

But Jeffreys, who was lucky to meet Andrea Dworkin, Gail Dines, and many other great feminists, keeps on fighting—and so will I.

If you're not or do not choose to be relationship material, the childfree lifestyle is the best option, too. Being single is great and should be celebrated, but—surprise!—it's often ridiculed, pitied, and stigmatized, just as is life without your own kids. Bella DePaulo is my favorite scholar and activist doing research in this field. She's written several books about happy singles and has an exciting blog. Many singles, she states, are happier than couples who have been together for years, whether sexually or in general. Nevertheless, singles in the United States face lots of discrimination, she writes. People in relationships enjoy *fixing* them *up*. Not being invited to events for couples is another example. DePaulo concedes that some actions against singles are well-meant or not that terrible, but in total the burden becomes quite heavy.

Mainstream aggression against those deviating from the norms takes remarkably similar forms. Many people seem to be unable to understand how one can choose being single or childfree or both. They genuinely think both or either is a fate nobody wants. Thankfully, DePaulo (and some others, like Professor Ashley English, who writes about the stigmatizing of unmarried women) have published more than one great book (e.g., DePaulo's *Singled Out: How Singles Are Stereotyped, Stigmatized, and Ignored, and Still Live Happily Ever After*) on this topic. They are showing that singles mostly have a great life, including interesting careers, hobbies, journeys, and friends. Who has time for Mr. Mediocre?

Single ladies often have to emphasize that they *do* like men—just like the childfree women, who must repeat *I do love children* in every second sentence if they don't want to be considered evil witches. Arthur Schopenhauer is on the singles' team, however. The German philosopher writes that being on your own is necessary to keep a sane mind, to develop your own thoughts, and to grow as a person. Only less intelligent people need others all the time, he thinks. So, let's be smart and courageous and defend our lifestyles, whether it's being single or childfree! We always make life easier for others in our group when speaking up on behalf of the marginalized ones.

3.5 Health Risks

For the sake of completeness, it's necessary to mention several health risks that pregnancy can provoke. I do this not to shame mothers' bodies but to inform those who can still escape. Women can die when they give birth: plain and simple. In Great Britain, 11 out of 100,000 mothers die each year, according to the WHO. That percentage is small, but it's not zero either. . . .

Even if you survive delivery, you often suffer from shock, diabetes, raised blood pressure, gestosis, low-lying placenta, or thrombosis. Further health threats are significant blood loss, infections, hereditary diseases, preterm delivery, stillbirth, prolapse of uterus/bladder, sagging breasts, hyperpigmentation of the face, hemorrhoids, flaccid musculature of your lower body, and so on. Some women also lose their hair and teeth afterward.

Even during late pregnancy and delivery, there can be challenges: complications in labor, anomalies of the baby's position or of the birth canal, problems with the umbilical cord. Embolism of the amniotic fluid can kill both mother and child. Thrombosis, stroke, or heart attacks are not uncommon among women who gave birth.

Then there are the minor, if embarrassing, side-effects of giving birth. These might be hair-growth in regions where you didn't have any before, more cellulite, constipation, and bigger, broader feet (cf. Healthway 2017). More seriously, you might suffer from chronic back pain or mental problems, such as postnatal depression, which is not only a biological, chemical phenomenon, but directly connected to cultural forces that mold women into mothers.

Research by the Baker Heart & Diabetes Institute in Melbourne, Australia (Baker 2019), found a link between multiple pregnancies (more than three) and stiffness in the heart, a disease discovered in the last ten years! But of course, every pregnancy affects your heart (and your whole body) negatively. More women than you'd expect find giving birth a traumatic experience and develop post-traumatic stress disorder (a condition also suffered by many prostitutes). A study led by the University of Sussex confirmed that these women noticed a declining satisfaction with their relationships, including sexual dysfunction and frequent arguments. They often blamed their partner for negative effects related to the traumatic incident, the childbirth itself (Griffiths 2019).

Not only do women's bodies suffer, their minds do too. No wonder annoyed childfree people sometimes use the terms *mombie* or *daddiot* for presumptuous parents who only care for their children—and nobody else. This is some kind of anti-social streak, which is maybe understandable in theory—taking into account the hormonal turmoil a pregnant woman goes through—but in practice, it irritates the hell out of you, nevertheless. A study found that serious brain remodeling does take place during pregnancy, making mothers more focused on their offspring (to put it mildly), ignoring the rest of the world (cf. Rauch 2017).

Of course, it's not only women who change negatively after procreation; men often become even more self-centered than before. One example is the German author Philipp Möller, who writes "funny" books (he's a popular mainstream scribbler). Born in 1980, he has three kids (one above replacement level, but let's remember, it's *German* children who are really important for this world) and published a book in 2019 titled *Isch geh Bundestag—Wie ich meiner*

Tochter versprach, die Welt zu retten. I Go to the Bundestag [Germany's Parliament]: *How I Promised My Daughter I'd Save the World* is a would-be witty account of a father (brave and noble, nothing to criticize) trying to make a difference—for *his* daughter, of course, because who else is there in this world who'd deserve his efforts? This is one more example of the utter selfishness parents display without a hint of embarrassment.

They do it all the time. At parent–teacher conferences, many of them ask about their child. Well, of course. But is it necessary to interrupt a teacher who is talking about their kid's whole class? Is it so unbearably irrelevant to hear about their child's classmates, about dynamics in this very classroom which affect the kid, too? For quite a lot of parents, this seems to be the case. Even people who just ponder the kid-question aren't always immune to egotistic moods, such as when they "publicly" say that they don't care about what they do to the environment by breeding, but that they do care about what they do to the child when they bring them into such an environment.

A case in point can be found in the article *Kinderlos—weil die Welt zu unsicher ist?* ("Childless—Because the World Is Not Safe Enough?"), published on November 24, 2019, in the Austrian newspaper *Die Presse*. The article featured several people wondering whether it was still a good idea to procreate in times of climate change. One person, Anja W., 31, said she was only interested in the effect this environment would have on *her* child. Figures. Anja is a coward who (unlike me, who openly and publicly fights for the childfree, with my name and face prominently displayed) is not interested in the big picture. When will people wake up? Why do they not realize that we just can't afford being selfish anymore? It will take a joint effort to keep this planet habitable for some years. We can't thrust our heads in the sand in 2022. It might have been possible in 1900, but given the present ecological emergency, it's no longer justifiable.

Of course, nobody wants a mother to neglect her baby, but does this have to result in the kind of completely reckless behavior that seems to be in vogue nowadays?

In the Middle Ages, the role of the king was of profound significance. The emblematic king had a marked sense of duty and responsibility, a kind of wonderful manliness and bravery, a patriarchal authority and wisdom. He was complete and perfect if he had a family: a wife and children (or at least one heir to the throne). If the king lacked kids, something had to be wrong, people would think—although there are many known examples of rulers (e.g., Heinrich and Kunegunde in the Holy Roman Empire of the eleventh century) who opted for a "childfree" life before such a notion even existed. Their subjects speculated about infertility, impotence, and many other medical problems this couple might have had.

This short excursion into history tells us a lot about our past—and about our present, as it is still (or rather, again) the case that childfree people are too often seen as somehow shady creatures who *must* have physical and or psychological handicaps. Yet, we aren't in the Middle Ages anymore. A man can still be manly, brave, responsible, and wise if he's not a father. And I would claim, even more so.

3.6 The Need for Childfree Spaces

According to clinical psychologist Diana Baumrind, there are four types of parenting: authoritarian, authoritative, permissive, and uninvolved. Whereas it was quite common to expect top-notch behavior from children in the nineteenth century, it has become increasingly popular to let them do whatever they want to do in the twenty-first.

A typical excuse for today's parents' permissive style is the commonplace *kids will be kids* and similar platitudes. It's also well-known—or at least it should be known, maybe some parents just ignore it—that children *need* education that deserves this name, that they *need* boundaries, and not some brainwashed mombie too pleased by the mere look of the new person she's created to actively educate this human being. And believe me, they *will* need it.

As a teacher I directly experience these daily parenting disasters. If you spend more than five minutes in any classroom you can easily tell which kid is a victim of the permissive parenting style and which isn't. Plenty of more or less amusing articles confirm my observations. You only need to read the title "Face It, Mom and Dad. I'm Not Special" by Jenny Dolan in the *New York Times* of November 22, 2019, to get the message.

So, it's not good for the child to be permitted to run wild all day. Innocent third parties suffer, if the parents can't be bothered. What about some (re)actions to counterbalance this horrible development in order to protect people from needless harm? More childfree spaces might help. If parents don't think it's necessary to educate their kids anymore, then we have to show them that this is completely inconsiderate toward people who want to get on with their lives peacefully.

A peaceful existence is why several childfree spaces came into existence in the first place. In the past, they weren't needed because parents either stayed at home or chose activities that pleased their kids (playing outside, going on a hike, swimming, cycling, etc.), instead of hanging out at cafés and restaurants all the time (which understandably bores the children to death).

Unfortunately, this seems to be an indispensable lifestyle nowadays. There are countless cafés catering to the needs of parents and little children, and nobody is going to criticize that. But the other way round? Outrage! If you want to be 100 percent sure of landing in an epic shitstorm, talk positively about a childfree café.

In Germany, an innkeeper received several death threats and an endless number of negative mails and fake reviews. Why this flood of hatred and negativity toward this innocent man, whose only crime had been to ban children under fourteen from his restaurant *in the evening*? His aim was to provide a peaceful, calm atmosphere for his guests who don't want to have their evening out destroyed by screaming, running little people. . . .

Rudolf Markl, sixty-five, runs the restaurant *Oma's Küche* (Grandma's Kitchen) on the beautiful island of Rügen in the Baltic Sea. In the articles about his decision that ran in August 2018, he explained that he wasn't anti-kid (the typical, most common allegation every childfree person has to deal with on almost a daily basis), but that the children's and parents' freedom couldn't disturb the freedom of other guests.

And that freedom is indeed disturbed when kids run amok in restaurants, throwing food, screaming at the top of their lungs, touching other guests and staff, and generally shredding everyone's nerves. Educating children is not the task of an innkeeper, as Markl pointed out correctly.

And even if we don't talk about toddlers desperately needing to be taught manners, I'm constantly amazed by other incidents that I encounter. One day at noon, I was enjoying my lunch break: the café I was sitting in was calm and relaxing, offering a place where you could really wind down after a stressful and noisy morning at school. The staff wasn't under particular pressure; there weren't that many guests around: an old man was peacefully reading his paper in a corner; two ladies were amusing themselves with their phones; and a college student was writing down notes on a sheet of paper with a book propped open in front of her. She was also sipping a latté.

Then all hell broke loose. It was a rather cold day, and all the windows and doors were shut, with the only blast of air coming when new guests walked in. This was the case now: a mother blocked the door for several minutes with her ginormous stroller, letting in bursts of chilly air. The student put on her jacket. When mother, stroller, and a toddler were finally in the building, the circus began. Although there were lots of empty places, it was obviously immensely hard for this family to choose. The toddler had to check each of them out individually, running like a demon from one seat to the next.

Finally, he decided on one. Layers after layers of clothing were removed by a huffing and puffing mother. This seemed to be hard work. Of course, one waitress was hit by a flying scarf when she was so imprudent as to pass too close to mother and sons.

After a quarter of an hour, they had settled, and the older boy started to cough. It wasn't an ordinary kind of cough, it sounded as if he was about to die from tuberculosis. The baby in the stroller then started to cry. And not just any "normal" sniffles, but full-blown howling. Without end. While mom had her essential-for-survival cup of coffee, her two kids were clearly not having a good time. Neither did the other guests in the café. The old man left, the two women exchanged worried glances, and several staff members looked pretty annoyed.

Why did this mother inflict this nightmare on all others present in this scene? It's really not easy to find a satisfying answer to this question. I'd be the first to argue that women are entitled to take a break from being a full-time mother. What isn't acceptable is to infringe on innocent third parties' rights and freedom while doing so. What about the fathers? Or professional people taking care of the kids if the exhausted parents need some time out?

Of course, the COVID pandemic changed this situation slightly, as many cafés had to close their doors. Generally, the measures against the virus led to a revival of the stay-at-home mom. There were indeed women who were happy being cooped up with petulant children, because the kids' father would come home directly after work, without stopping at his health club, a pub, a shop, or in some cases, a brothel. Traditional family values suddenly seemed to matter again. Finally, it was considered a cause of celebration to sit at home all day, playing with the kids, doing chores, and nothing more.

Of course, many mothers also complained, especially when their housing wasn't appropriate. Yet, while mothers' fates were considered during lockdowns, other women didn't seem to matter. What about single women, lesbians, little girls, and seniors? If we take women's problems seriously, we must care for all women, and not only those who decided to give birth.

Today's feminism often is a disappointingly reduced version, distilled to one question: How can we make a mother's burden lighter? This can be one question of many, but nowadays it seems to be the only one—and that reminds us of the Nazis again, when the *Vaterländische Front* published the *Mütterzeitung* (mothers' newspaper), featuring a breastfeeding mom not interested in anything other than breeding as many new soldiers as possible. During their horrible reign, the support for couples who desired children increased significantly, whereas taxes for the childfree/childless were raised.

In this context, many laws seem to be designed to make motherhood more attractive to women. If you work at a school, for example, you don't have to show up when you're pregnant as soon as the flu season starts, while you receive *full* pay. This is very unfair, especially if you consider that fragile people whose immune system is chronically impaired don't receive such preferential treatment. It's supposed to benefit the women: but in reality it's never about the women, it's about the unborn children. The woman's worth is defined by her "capacity" to give birth to new subjects/soldiers/consumers/. . . . This bears a strong resemblance to "pro-lifers" when we talk about abortion: to veil their anti-feminist agenda, they present their goals as "pro-women." But it's really pro-uterus, the female personality who owns it is irrelevant. If women only deserve being treated well as future or potential mothers, this can never be feminist; instead, it's the opposite: pure patriarchal ideology. This must be pointed out because, in the backlash, more and more women are buying into this nonsense. They feel flattered; suddenly, they finally seem to matter. But they don't: female incubators matter.

4

POLITICS

4.1 Right-Wing Parties and Their Leaders

Consider the far-right German politicians of the Alternative for Germany (AfD). Hermann L. Gremliza, the late publisher of the left-wing monthly *Konkret*, correctly called them a Nazi party. Italian minister of the interior, Matteo Salvini; former US President Donald Trump; or Hungarian Prime Minister Viktor Orbán, and many other representatives of the new Right. In times when they embrace so-called family values—the typical nuclear family—real anti-fascism has to go on the attack.

Is there a connection between right-wing extremist policies and the obsession to give birth? What about the hardcore anti-feminist approach of all new Right policies, including that of Michael Klonovsky, a political advisor to AfD, who wrote that a "woman who did not give birth has failed the very core of her existence"? This kind of patriarchal hatred of women's self-determination is familiar from the times of Nazi Germany and its obsession with the birth rate. I'll repeat: women who gave birth to four or more children were awarded a special cross by Nazi Germany—the "mother cross."

Nowadays, we have to endure statesmen who are openly anti-feminist. They exist in many countries, and not only in the United States. In Italy for instance, former premier Silvio Berlusconi was renowned for his so-called Bunga Bunga parties and interesting quotes concerning women: it was women's fault if they were raped, the head of state said more than once, because Italian women are so beautiful. Victim-blaming was an unknown concept for Berlusconi, who regularly chose women from poor regions (usually young enough to be his grand-daughters) to appear at his side at public events. His own daughter Eleonora lives the life of a devoted mom. There it is again: the ancient dichotomy of saint and harlot. The political right knows only these two types of women. It makes sense that their members are often antisemitic homophobes who find nothing wrong with prostitution and hunting.

Sadly, though, this highly restrictive pattern of femininity does not stop at party boundaries. Anti-feminist resentment knows neither time nor political inclination. One might think that it's only the conservatives of every country who favor traditional values, such as the nuclear family. A certain tendency confirms this trend, but in general, every party program puts a special emphasis on family. Breeding has to be encouraged, first and foremost, if we talk about right- or left-wingers. Why this obsession with their own people?

Even people who consider themselves Marxists often find it necessary to procreate, viewing anti-natalism as some kind of bourgeois ideology. I suppose that the proletariat must make new proletarians so that the revolutionary class doesn't die out. Yes, children are receptacles of all the things their parents want to put into them, but these kids also join the ranks of consumers. They can't help serving Capital.

So, it's clear that every party is inherently pro-natalist. The politicians want the parents' votes and as most adults are parents, every politician has to be immensely child-friendly. Whether it's fake or not, nobody cares; but politicians must flatter parents, otherwise the career in question will never take off. One shouldn't overdo it, though, thinking of Joe Biden's kissing of little girls a bit too fondly (North 2019).

Friedrich Nietzsche wrote in his famous book *Also sprach Zarathustra*: "Viel zu Viele werden geboren: für die Überflüssigen ward der Staat erfunden!" (or, as I would translate it, "Way too many are born: for the superfluous the state was invented.") This might give us a clue. Each state needs people to perpetuate the existing hierarchical structures. So, having children is always an act of affirming the status quo, including all the atrocities we are faced with. It's not surprising that with the current backlash, German birth rates are rising. People *want* to be conservative and make their very own contribution to the preservation of institutions they consider sacred. Each and every government worldwide applauds every mating pair and shovels bonus after bonus upon them. Yet it should be clear there are natural limits to growth of any kind (economical, concerning population, etc.) on a finite planet.

Of course, it is mainly the political right that praises breeders more than anything, because they need their offspring as cheap cannon fodder—a connection many people just don't want to see. Capitalism in general needs as many children as possible—who else is going to be tomorrow's consumer?

You can observe a shift to the right throughout Europe. Many books deal with this phenomenon, but they usually focus on other priorities considered dangerous, such as their anti-immigration policy. But even if we talk about this aspect of population, there's a direct link to the main topic of this book: in order to keep refugees and other immigrants out, the right needs more native children. They deny the poorer parts of the world our first-world conditions on purpose, using anti-feminist strategies to kill two birds with one stone: make the native women breed, then we can keep the others out. ("BUILD THE WALL!" Is a slogan not only Trump fans shout, but also right-wing Hungarians—they want refugees to be kept out.) To the right, breeding also means that women have a "useful" occupation while the men can continue their warmongering undisturbed.

A myriad of texts about Trump have stressed the sexist, antisemitic, racist, vulgar behavior of the former American president. Not many have outlined, however, that men like him always have a large family. They consider their genes especially valuable and in the typically narcissistic way of thinking, these men are convinced it's their duty to sire as many children as possible. Similar to the Italian mafia, they have a strong tendency to prioritize their own clan—in every respect. God wants them to multiply, too, they argue, although there's also a right-wing minority that doesn't make religious reasons first and foremost in their justification.

Such new crusaders are, for example, Salvini in Italy, Orbán in Hungary, the whole AfD party in Germany, Beata Mazurek in Poland, and many more. They typically encourage families to have more than one or two children, subsidizing their lifestyle heavily: massive tax breaks, special loans, even a van (in Hungary; similar in Italy). Tendencies like that also exist in the Netherlands and Austria.

Katalin Novák, a member of Hungary's right-wing Fidesz party and Minister of State for Family, Youth, and International Affairs, has three children herself who feature prominently. The daughter is called Kata (and they say it isn't about producing a mini-me!). The Nováks even invited me to Budapest, by the way—probably as the demon itself. Of course, I didn't meet them. As the anti-fascist slogan says: WHEN IS A GOOD TIME TO TALK TO THE NAZIS? NEVER.

Poland also introduced a huge child benefit for big families. Of course, abortion is a real thorn in the flesh of politicians who want ever more kids. Since January 2021, the Poles have lived under a ban on virtually all abortions. Repression is also occurring for homosexuals or feminists—or in fact, any kind of dissidents who don't support these leaders' fascist concepts.

The German AfD wants to abolish Gender Studies, and their attitude toward gays and lesbians is no surprise either: AfD functionary Björn Höcke has said that you must tolerate them—in the sense of putting up with them, but nothing more. In fact, it's not acceptable to the right. They've made clear that homosexual couples definitely don't belong in schoolbooks, for instance.

It was the Nazis who introduced child benefits in 1935. Of course, Mother's Day was also a concept they adored and promoted, and many mothers still celebrate it (well, if it makes them happy having a one-day break from the chores and receiving crappy paintings from their offspring. . .). Lots of people even think the Nazis *invented* Mother's Day, which isn't surprising, because it's exactly their ideology.

In Germany, it's more conservative mothers who find this day important. Some modern moms don't care, and even consider it ridiculous, pointing out that one day doesn't make a difference and that they'd prefer more help in the household, instead of a present and a dinner out once a year. Meanwhile in 2016, the Polish right-wing party Prawo i Sprawiedliwość passed a bill that guarantees women who deliberately decide to give birth to a severely ill or disabled child a single payment of a thousand Euros.

Anyone who thinks of Verona, Italy, probably pictures Romeo and Juliet's balcony or some opera taking place there. But in March 2019, a gruesome procession conquered the streets of this lovely, little town: the *World Congress of Families* was held there, thanks to activities of Matteo Salvini's right-wing *Lega* (a.k.a. the Northern League). His party openly battles abortion (and physicians who perform them), appealing to people's religious conscience. As a result, seventy percent of Italian doctors don't offer this service anymore, with up to ninety percent in the more conservative South no longer carrying them out.

Given this situation one should muse upon this further—if you really want to procreate and by doing so help the new right build their 21ˢᵗ-century fascist states. The individuals in such a state are *never* important, they just need numbers to outdo their neighbors and competitors.

Of course, every government bribes people to have large families—staying in power and bowing to the economy are always more important than saving the environment. Do they really not get that *every* problem is easier to solve if there are fewer people? Even Sir Peter Scott, founder of WWF, had to admit that his organization had failed. The WWF had wanted to save endangered species from extinction. Somehow, that didn't work. If they'd put all the money into condoms, he observed, they might have done something good. Right he is.

So, one very valuable measure to influence population growth in a way that helps our environment is the reduction of child benefits. But what is happening? The opposite. In Germany, in June 2020, every family received 300 euros per child—as a present. Government officials said that families should use this amount to go shopping. This is neither a joke nor a lie. Yes, it did enrage people without kids, and it also enraged some parents, who wrote to me saying they didn't need nor want the money, and that the government should have supported other projects instead. One mother quipped she needed the cash for earplugs. . . . How funny! What about *educating* your kids so they aren't a nuisance for parents, neighbors, and teachers?

Regrettably, child benefits are to be raised again (*and* families' tax breaks will become even bigger), at least in Germany. Bavaria recently passed a new law to support childless couples' IVF treatments, with four-digit grants per couple. If you think globally, this gets really depressing. Imagine how many children who already exist could be saved from horrible fates like starvation, illness, childhood marriage, and genital mutilation if the money were directed toward them?

People shouldn't listen to hopelessly backward/right-wing government representatives anymore when they reiterate that more and more native babies are the solution to all our problems—when the opposite is true. We need *fewer* children in each and every country, first and foremost in the global North.

Foreigners coming to Germany are surprised that such a high amount of child benefit is splashed out: an Englishman in Germany told me he received more than 400 euros for his two kids (at home he got much less). This is one reason why German birth rates rise and English ones decline. Especially detrimental is the support of ever bigger families: the more kids a couple has, the more money it receives—exponentially. There are indeed people who go on breeding in order to get by on the huge amount of child benefits they receive every month. Is this something we should support in 2022?

4.2 Backlash

In 1991, Susan Faludi's *Backlash* listed patriarchal reactions (starting in the 1980s) to the first real feminist success stories. Several strategies could be observed. One of the most popular and effective is the defamation of feminist pioneers and the negative portrayal of women who don't fulfill male imperatives (concerning one's personal appearance, for instance).

Defamation and negative portrayal still work. More and more German women let themselves be persuaded that motherhood is a *sine qua non*. Journalist Bascha Mika (and many others) found that even mothers *who earn more* than the fathers spend more time doing chores and caring for the kids (Mika 2017, p. 116)!

There once was a glorious time when being a (radical) feminist meant not reproducing because reproduction was the core patriarchal imperative. Unfortunately, these golden years are way in the past. My own mom was ridiculed by several acquaintances when she announced her pregnancy in 1979. *Ah, the feminist, finally giving in to patriarchal norms*, they would laugh.

Maybe we should remember those genuine feminist values and celebrate them again by empowering women who go against the grain instead of giving in, fulfilling what society expects of them, only because they own ovaries.

Nowadays, even weddings aren't about the happy couple anymore; group photos feature babies and toddlers prominently, as if children were the only reason for two loving people to get married. It's absolutely crucial to separate these two aspects: we're not in the nineteenth century anymore, when it was vital for a pregnant woman to be married if she didn't want to end up an outcast. You can have kids out of wedlock. Please don't destroy the romance of a marriage by intertwining it with reproduction. Some people find this offensive.

An acquaintance told me she wanted her wedding to be childfree. Of course, she couldn't go through with that, otherwise her mother would have had virtually nobody to talk to for the rest of her life and my acquaintance didn't want to do this to her. That's fair enough, but this story is immensely sad. Shouldn't a wedding be about the bride and her groom and their wishes, dreams, and desires? What do patriarchal norms have to do with that?

You can argue that marriage itself is a conservative institution that should be rejected, along with giving birth to several kids. Fine. Yet there are romantic people who like the idea of marrying, while disliking the idea of reproduction. That should be acceptable too.

Some very traditional women dream of nothing else than getting married in white, in church of course, and becoming mothers. Let me repeat: a woman can have so much more in her life than limiting herself to the domestic sphere. It's the backlash that makes one unhappy because there was a time when more women realized that caring for a family isn't as rewarding as it's presented everywhere.

Today's pseudo- or even anti-feminism, disguised as real feminism, asks one single question: How can we make mothers' lives more comfortable? I challenge this. This is not a feminist question. A genuine feminist is concerned to destroy the cage we're supposed to live in, rather than decorating it so we like our prison better.

If you're not convinced yet, look at the entities and groups applauding pregnant women: capitalists; politicians, especially the ones belonging to the right wing; any religious institution; the army; parents, friends, relatives, neighbors, colleagues. . . . This is why our society is called pro-natalist. Virtually any institution will gush over another human being about to be delivered. The economy needs as many consumers as possible; the politicians with their veiled fascist agenda need as many *native* babies and new people as possible; each faith/religion needs as many devotees as possible—the list could go on *ad infinitum*. It's obvious, though, that these masses of new people are not interesting as individuals; they are only important in numbers. That much should be clear.

Conservative parents who pressure their own children into providing grandchildren are unfortunately relatively common. Are they crazy? Have they not realized that the ecological situation has changed drastically? That there might also be millions of other reasons not to choose this traditional path already trodden by billions of others?

Some people reject reproducing existing structures—over and over again. "Settling down" and having kids is such a boring way of leading your life—exactly the way one's parents did, exactly the way society expects people (especially women) to behave. It's a pity that so many let themselves be lured into a life of dependence.

Many young mothers have personally told me (and some have also written about it) that as soon as their lives entailed caring for one or more little children, they automatically ended up with most of the chores and some kind of subjection to their men. How does that happen?

Christina Mundlos is a German author who adds more flavors to a phenomenon that gained worldwide recognition under the label REGRETTING MOTHERHOOD. Orna Donath, a sociologist from Israel, portrayed a bunch of mothers who all agreed: they wouldn't do it again (Televisor Troika, n.d.).

The 2018 movie *Life of the Party* is a comedy, and while you can't expect real criticism of procreation in such a film, it's surprising how honestly certain negative aspects of motherhood are portrayed. Melissa McCarthy as Deanna ("Mom") talks in a funny yet poignant way about sagging breasts, hips that don't support backpacking any more, and scars and pains due to her Caesarean operation. She maintains an impressive body positivity, though, which she also passes on to her new friends by praising the legs of a fellow student, the face of another, and the hair of a third one. The message is clear: be proud of what you have. Don't waste time and energy longing for assets you don't have. A little drawback is the makeover she lets her daughter inflict upon her: no glasses please, and no "mom-pullovers."

Much more important than superficial aspects, though, are her "lost" twenty years! Her daughter is present when she admits it, so her mother quickly clarifies that she's proud and happy to have had her, but that *her* own life hadn't been a priority during these two decades, which placed her at a severe economic disadvantage.

In real life, women like Deanna sometimes end up on *Snapped*, an American crime show that has run since 2004, and highlights women accused of murder. Interestingly, the biographies of these women almost always start with some version of "She had everything, a husband, two children, a house, and a dog." Yet they commit murder. Maybe "everything" isn't the best for every woman, what about less is more? There are so many mothers who prove that motherhood isn't for everyone and that it can end in a disaster if you let yourself be pushed in this direction.

Life of the Party fights against ageism, too: Deanna has an affair with a very young guy (you don't have to be Brigitte Macron to do this) and she faces ageist remarks from bullies. Her revenge is to be the life of the party—vibrant, amusing and with absolutely contagious energy. And she manages to graduate. There are indeed lessons to be learned from this movie: never become dependent on a man. If you have a child, make sure to keep your own interests alive: job, friendships, hobbies. Don't accept discrimination of any kind.

It's clear that mothers don't express much solidarity with one another. Mundlos describes how they envy and even fight each other—in a sometimes open, but much more often latent way. Cyberbullying is a problem not only students have to face, but it seems that many mothers also share this experience. There are lots of websites like *Scary Mommy* (the name says it all). It seems to be impossible to be a mother without belonging to at least ten online groups, allegedly offering support and empowerment, while selling to gullible moms goods they'll never need and contributing to their insecurity by offering "advice," which often leads to pressures of all kinds. Some of these sites describe themselves as a "guilt-free place for moms." Well, mothers often talk about their feelings of inadequateness *after* having spent time on these sites.

Leslie Kern admits that life is great for mothers in Canada, especially in the cities, but not in the suburbs or countryside, and that women around the world are confronted by much harder conditions. She acknowledges that the mom network is rather superficial. Watching movies together while looking after another mom's child does not necessarily mean that the two women are close friends. She relates that with one of her acquaintances, she regularly jokes around, for example saying they'll get rooms in the same retirement home. Somehow, stories like these always make this reader cringe. It's so thinly veiled that these two ladies try desperately to be "cool" moms, not expecting anything from their kids, while secretly hoping that their children *will* care for them later, thus providing an opportunity to boast again: "Well, *my* son/daughter doesn't send me off."

This goes well with Kern's condescending attitude toward those courageous women who do venture out by themselves. She describes the pitying looks they receive when they enter a restaurant on their own, not expecting anyone. Yet she complains about how often her child had disrespected her privacy by following her into the shower, bathtub, or restroom. For women, it seems to be a choice between the devil and the deep blue sea.

One of the great wonders is why so many people don't even consider adoption or different types of close contact with children. French president Emmanuel Macron, for example, didn't sire any kids, but he shares his life with the three children (and their offspring) of his wife, Brigitte. He once even called them his *children of the heart*. Genes aren't the important aspect about parenting, he's absolutely right there; it's about love and caring. Why do you have to be responsible for somebody's physical existence when you can alleviate their problems?

In Maëlle Brun's biography of Brigitte, you read about the many negative comments Brigitte has had to endure ever since she started dating the young man who'd later become president and her husband. "Cougars" aren't judged lightly. Everyone remembers the Trumps' meeting with the French First Couple, when the

American—of course—had to comment on Brigitte's impeccable appearance. Clichés about well-dressed French women seem to be true in this case, since the media agreed that the older woman had more taste and style than Melania. Nevertheless, why was it the women's physical appearance which was under so much scrutiny? Why were they compared in such a typically misogynistic way? Why are women's clothes always much more important and interesting than men's?

One implication is that superficial aspects are more relevant for other people's judgment of her. Casual Friday or Dress Down Tuesday are easy for men: you just don some shorts, throw on a T-shirt, slip on flip-flops and you're done. For women, nail polish, shaved legs and armpits, a well-groomed hairstyle, make-up, and so on are still procedures to be considered. There is always the fear that you might start your period earlier than usual (some women never have regular menstruations, due to hormonal imbalances), which makes many girls and women feel uncomfortable in white clothes.

Scotland was progressive enough to introduce free sanitary tampons. In most other countries, this is still a faraway dream, and will be as long as people continue to talk about *the curse*, using that very word. Such an attitude has to change quickly and completely. In every school, girls and women clutch tampons as if they were dirty secrets before quietly sneaking to the restroom. A period is nothing to be ashamed of! That's why there are YouTube videos featuring three young employees talking openly about menstruation. Result: the men present grimace and saunter off. Hopefully, more men (young and old) change their attitude toward the female period. Cool guys even offer their women tea, a massage, especially kind words, etc.—and it doesn't threaten their masculinity at all.

Women also need to have the courage to be more visible. Jasmine Alicia Carter and Yapci Ramos make art out of their own menstrual blood to draw attention to a natural phenomenon that is socially taboo. A woman wearing a white dress sat in front of me during a concert last summer and when she rose from her chair, a prominent red blotch decorated her dress. The poor woman almost died of shame. Well, it wasn't as if she had been incontinent, and even those things happen. We need more tolerance! We should celebrate every month we survived without getting pregnant. There's no reason to hide.

Shame has traditionally accompanied the female body (and most of its functions). In the Western intellectual tradition, Aristotle started it and countless self-proclaimed authorities of all trades have followed, explaining over and over again why women are inferior creatures. Even Kant, considered oh-so-progressive and egalitarian, was writing about the mind of *man*. He made special efforts to show that girls require a different education, suited to their lesser mental abilities. He was extremely paternalistic and seemed to think that women were more like pets or children (it's Ancient Greek tradition, placing the woman somewhere near the enslaved or an animal). There's no place for such thinking in the twenty-first century.

Returning to Brigitte Macron: Whereas it's perfectly normal for men to have a much younger wife, especially when he's in a position of power, it's highly unusual for such a man to have a much older wife. So, Brigitte suffers a double double standard. She is attacked with sexist *and* ageist remarks, often combined. It doesn't help that she's a mother, since that fact is also used against her—leaving the father of her children for another man is something for which no mother will be forgiven.

So unusual is the Brigitte–Emmanuel phenomenon that some have insinuated (and this conspiracy doesn't only come from Russia) that Macron must be gay and is using Brigitte as a cover. The president himself reacted to this allegation, clarifying that he wasn't homophobic and would live openly as a gay man if he was, and that such statements offended his wife. It's pathetic that, for some people, having a much older wife is unimaginable and a story must be invented to explain it.

The Italian politician Teresa Bellanova, born in 1958, is another famous person directly affected by the lethal combination of sexism and ageism. She is farming minister in the government of Prime Minister Giuseppe Conte. She's not thin, wears her hair short, and gets caught in regular shitstorms because of this (and her choice of outfits). When she was sworn in, she wore a blue dress one could describe as old-fashioned, but she said that it had fit her mood that day perfectly and people should prepare themselves to see her in orange, if she feels like it. That attitude is terrific, but not everyone copes that well.

Silvio Berlusconi's partners, who wear blond highlights and/or extensions, high heels, and clothes originally designed for teenagers are also criticized. Differently, of course, but as an aging woman you just can't get it right, and not only in Italy.

Fortunately, the phenomenon of WHIP (Women Who are Hot and Intelligent) is gaining popularity, and there are progressive people all around the world who realize that age isn't the most important feature of a woman's desirability, and that maturity can be positive. Why should a woman's maturity and experience (traditionally considered great assets in a man!) be of no value? Why should these features make them unattractive, while enhancing a man's charm? We all remember the kind, lovely, old wizards and nasty witches of fairy tales, but it's high time we left the land of make-believe.

It's crucial to discard the notion that women are mere decorations for wealthy men, although there'll always be couples like the Trumps who endorse this concept. Luckily, Vice-President Kamala Harris is a role model already throughout the world. With two stepchildren, she is quite progressive in living childfree but caring for children too.

Popular culture doesn't help as much as it should to break stereotypes. Rap music and the videos accompanying the tracks unfortunately often feature women as mere objects. Scantily dressed young women usually dance around one "powerful" guy, who is often a) older, b) fatter, c) fully dressed, and d) the only male. The lyrics regularly feature abusive and derogatory terms concerning women in general. One woman, however, is above criticism: the performer's mother.

Literature doesn't help either. Most "chick lit" is about the heroine's irrational fears about turning thirty or forty (to be even older seems unthinkable!). Yes, there is Mike Gayle and his novel *Turning Forty*, but the problems an ageing man has to face don't compare. The main worry facing Matt, Gayle's protagonist, is the new shed he harps on about, his symbol of settling down and becoming boring. Matt doesn't feel the immense pressure women are under: How will they be able to find the right guy to start a family with when the clock has already been ticking for quite a while?

Time's inevitability for women has few exceptions in literature. One comes from the Italian novelist Marilù Oliva, author of *Le sultane*, a book from 2014, which depicts three female retirees, who behave in partly shocking, partly amusing ways. Some of their quirks are also so touching that you almost cry. One of the women uses a tea bag three times—you want to hug her! For two of the women, sex isn't relevant anymore. But one of them feels her passion rekindled by a muscular, young Black man. Some readers might characterize her behavior as exactly like a "dirty old man." Yet the storyline is highly subversive, mainly because an older woman lusting after a younger man remains such a taboo.

Oliva's book should be translated into every language, because it's so well written that you feel the three retirees are real characters, neighbors or friends you know. And the book increases the visibility of older women. Novels like *Le sultane* show that ageist and sexist stereotypes are nonsense, and that there's hope for older women, whether in fiction or in real life.

In *The Change: Women, Aging and the Menopause* (1993), Germaine Greer writes that older women shouldn't let the media pressurize them into having sex if it's not what *they* want. She has a point, and you often hear sad stories about dry vaginas that are only used by their owners to stop their husbands leaving them, and not because *they* are in the mood. On that score, if we believe Bill Bytheway, it's "the sight of the older un-self-conscious naked body and the possible reality of completely private sexual behavior which challenges so many cherished beliefs about dirty old men and frustrated spinsters" (pp. 84–85).

Many older women think it's their duty to "keep up" with younger ones (for the same reason). I say, *No!* If your man only fancies superficialities, he's no use anyway! And it's also his duty to appeal to his wife, and not (only) the other way around! How many unattractive seniors complain quite openly and often about the looks of their wives. One always wants to ask if they've had the opportunity to look in a mirror lately.

Pornography teaches young and old men that women are always up for it; that it's not necessary to seduce them, all you're required to do is stick a penis into every available orifice. That's why we still need radical feminism. While many "modern" types of feminists find nothing wrong with porn, radical feminism rejects it, as it usually degrades women. I've written an entire book on this topic, but I'll sum it up in one sentence: Porn, just like prostitution, is detrimental to women and eventually to men, too, even if they often don't realize it or only when it's too late. (There are porn-addicted young men who can't have ordinary sex anymore, because they are dysfunctional or need ever more explicit porn to get in the mood.)

If we want free lust and real equality, we have to get rid of sexist "adult entertainment." This is all male privilege. Of course, men have been used to this kind of entitlement and arrogance all their lives, so why should they give it up now. Never mind! It's the old white heterosexual man who has the power. Let's set out to take it from him!

In *Prime* (2005), a movie definitely worth watching (especially if you like Uma Thurman and/or Meryl Streep), 37-year-old Rafi (Uma Thurman) falls in love with a 23-year-old guy, who is not only Jewish but also her therapist's son. Those aren't the only obstacles either. The age gap is the major problem, sadly linked to Rafi's desire to procreate. Rafi breaks it off with her lovely young lover, because she doesn't want to force him into the role of a father, which, she reckons, would be too much for him.

I was furious when the movie ended like this! Why not write a screenplay in which Rafi enjoys her childfree life with her young man? And why not have a baby with a young man, if this urge is stronger than everything else? It's now possible to freeze one's eggs, although it's usually neglected or ignored that not only do ovaries age, but sperm quality decreases with every year. However, old or ancient fathers face no or almost no criticism, while every mother who is older than forty (sometimes older than thirty or thirty-five!) receives remarks, comments, and advice she doesn't really need. For some men, it seems unbearable to watch an older mom and her small child. Why? Because it clashes so harshly with their traditional Madonna-and-child-images? Because they want to see young firm breasts feeding the baby?

One of the big battles is whether to work or not when the kid is still young. In Germany, many mothers don't work at all when their kids are small. Later on, they only work part-time. So, it's "logical" that they do everything in the household. Isn't it?

The phenomenon of earning significantly less than their male peers—a gender wage gap known in every country and due to several reasons and not only the rearing of children—leads to poverty among the elderly and low(er) self-esteem in younger women. Lower self-esteem leads to more obedience in the internal power structure of the couple, who might have started out on equal footing.

Many mothers not only depend on their children's father financially, but also emotionally because their social contacts are suddenly quite limited to other mothers, euphemistically labeled "friends," or one's own mother. Before giving birth, these women had real friends and colleagues, and interesting events to attend. Instead, the new mother has lots of little, repetitive jobs throughout the day and is exhausted at the end of it. Yet many report that they aren't particularly happy and definitely not up for sex. Later on, they complain about other mothers to make themselves feel better. So why does society go to great lengths to make sure every woman falls into this trap?

The situation bears resemblance to the discourse about prostitution. The radical feminist approach is abolition. A sexist system based upon the exploitation of women shouldn't have a place in today's emancipated society. The same applies to motherhood: Why bear shackles if we can also be free? Why subject yourself to typical patriarchal control over female bodies, which seem only to be of a bit of interest as long as they are fertile? Afterward, all women are mere grandmothers (no matter if they actually have any grandchildren) and pushed into asexuality. Not every woman is eager to accept this limited range of roles.

Of course, a strong connection exists between the omnipresent degradation of old people and the blatant misogyny promoted by people like Trump. Old men (especially white, heterosexual, middle- or upper-class—if we choose to employ such terms) still have a lot of power in this world. Women, however, are (apart from a very small percentage) generally irrelevant or only relevant in the very restricted private sphere.

Hair color is one aspect that tells us a lot about the deplorable state our society is in. Old men can go gray or bald—and it's not a problem. Yes, we are superficial, but only when it comes to women. Men don't have to shave, use make-up, or dye their hair, they seem perfect the way they are; yet somehow, it's never really okay for women to present a (completely) natural look. Naomi Wolf's *The Beauty Myth* is still very relevant, more than thirty years after it was first published. In fact, it's even more so, given the new methods (seemingly invented every day) by which women mutilate their perfectly healthy female bodies.

The French writer and journalist Sophie Fontanel wrote *Une Apparition*, an entire book (that I highly recommend) about going gray. She became more visible when she stopped dyeing her hair. It's even more of a statement if you never start this process that only costs time and money and isn't good for your health anyway. It's a popular myth that you look older when you don't keep up the illusion of youth and fertility for the patriarchy.

Anne Kreamer also wrote about this phenomenon in her book *Going Gray*. Can one be an attractive female if you don't dye your hair? What an embarrassing question to ask! The perception has fortunately begun to change. In Germany, gray was named the "hair color trend of 2019," and more and more women find the courage to accept natural changes that have nothing to do with loss of attractiveness. On the contrary! Some choose extremely artificial, harsh colors.

Yet the fear of looking old or ugly when not dyeing your hair is still depressingly common. An otherwise pretty cool lesbian artist, about thirty years old, went nuts during lockdown 2021. She complained about her graying hairline, and almost sobbed that there were no hairdressers around. She had a date and wanted to "look good" for the hot woman she was to meet. I told her she looked perfect the way she was, even more interesting and alluring.

For those who fear they can be perceived as less beautiful, I can only say: many, many people wrote to me following my book's publication and several of them mentioned my gray hair—which is not typical of a woman in her late thirties—all of them very positively. The vast majority were men. Some even wrote: *What I like best about your looks is your hair color.* My activism is about political issues, but I didn't mind these compliments.

Hair color is also affected by colorism and the pursuit of whiteness. Why did Colombian singer Shakira suddenly appear as a blonde? Why did the Belgian soccer star Fellaini, whose thick natural black curls have always amazed me, change his looks and dye his hair blond, which didn't suit him at all? The German-Syrian novelist Rafik Schami confirms this is a recent trend: in the past, he notes, women dyed their hair many different colors, but gradually there was one single color they went for: blond.

What about certain hairstyles? Hamburg-born anthropologist Abina Ntim explains that the struggles of Black people are devalued if someone like the white celebrity Kim Kardashian wears cornrows simply to attract attention. Black women lost their jobs because of their cornrows, Ntim says. This dimension shouldn't be neglected.

Cultural appropriation is also a problem if you think about the fashion for hijabs, which ignores the subjugation in the Arab world of thousands of women, who were often imprisoned when fighting for their right to walk bareheaded through the streets.

It's not only about hair: why do Asian women (and some men) have operations to make their eyes look bigger, more European? Why do Iranian women (and some men) undergo plastic surgery to reduce the size of their noses?

A bald head for women is even worse than gray hair. For men, it's absolutely all right not to sport any hair; television shows talk about Hollywood's most attractive bald men, and Bruce Willis and Vin Diesel are even considered heartthrobs. Women who lose their hair (and they sometimes do, due to various medical conditions) could never walk around like men do in this case: nonchalant, feeling desired. Usually, they do everything to hide this condition by wearing headgear or a wig. There are some fierce rebel women who shave their heads, like some men, but they are a tiny minority.

Does this liberation from gray hair have anything to do with being childfree? Of course it does! It's all about feminism, about being a female individual, and about challenging patriarchal norms. We have wonderful shoulders on which to stand. Susan Sontag told us in "The Double Standard of Aging," an essay she wrote for the September 23, 1972 edition of *The Saturday Review*, how aging is okay for men, whereas women are punished for it. That was half a century ago!

Sontag is not alone. Famous feminists like Barbara Macdonald, Betty Friedan, and of course Simone de Beauvoir wrote about aging women. (De Beauvoir considered a life without any sexual activity useless. Studies show that, luckily, there are women who don't share this opinion.) Many different and interesting perspectives can be found in their publications. In general, age or aging doesn't feature prominently in modern-day Gender Studies, which is quite sad. Older women thus become even more invisible and marginalized. It's fatal that so many books deal with mothers, but not with women who are not mothers and/or older than fifty. This absence feeds the vicious circle: women who can reproduce are interesting, so old age is dreaded, and young women tend to become mothers out of fear. If we didn't ignore older women, we might avoid feeling fated to give birth.

It's little kids who tell you that women don't have hairy legs or gray hair—not knowing about their mother's efforts to keep up this illusion without stubble or stray threads of any kind. Coronavirus and everything that followed has shown how important hair is for some. I saw women rushing through the streets, wearing hats, headscarves, or bandanas to cover their graying roots! To be fair, some also grabbed the opportunity to finally stop dyeing their hair. How did we as a society get to a point where women are ashamed to show their faces without (properly) dyed hair?

That's why we need Germaine Greer's *The Change*—unfortunately still relevant almost thirty years later. Women always groom themselves to please men, she argues. Dyeing your hair, fasting all the time, having cosmetic surgery, exercising excessively—all those habits support patriarchal norms that want women to spend all their time, energy, and money on fulfilling them.

Instead of hoping that the children will remember you in your dotage and sometimes pop around when you live in a retirement home, it may be worthwhile to invest your energy differently while you still possess it. As I already explained: studies have shown that old people without kids and grandkids aren't lonelier than their peers who did reproduce. Not much of a surprise there! The childfree people had time to cultivate real friendships and close relationships with many different people, whereas parents only cared for their offspring for almost twenty years.

A reproach I often hear concerns retirement income. *Don't we need children for that?* And I'm the cynic?! Swiss economist Reiner Eichenberger regularly states that kids shouldn't be used this way. Furthermore, he writes, a child costs the community more than it will ever contribute. An unconditional basic income is a solution many people and some political parties are discussing, but it's high time we came up with alternatives to providing for our old age. But if the bleak climate prospects come true, we won't need a pension anyway, given we'll have no air to breathe.

4.3 Adoring the Child

French philosopher Élisabeth Badinter has written many books about motherhood, pointing out that there is no such thing as an *innate* maternal instinct; it's merely a social construction to keep women where they "belong." Society glorifies motherhood to lure as many women as possible into the trap. Lots of German women work part-time, do most of the domestic chores, spend time trying to keep up their appearance—and then break down in exhaustion. Their male partners, on the other hand, simply go about enjoying their lives.

Badinter points out that *l'enfant roi* ultimately serves to suppress women. Bowing before one's own child as if they were royalty is a modern phenomenon in France, Germany, and apparently all countries in the West. Mothers are supposed to put themselves second and fulfill their child's every whim. Apart from the educational disaster such subservience leads to, it can't be healthy for the woman. Part of this mother cult is of course breast-feeding, and Badinter is surprised by how willingly women take part in this scheme. Everybody seems to do it, which is why the French philosopher calls childfree women *revolutionary*.

Badinter mentions differences between German and French mothers (the situation is not as difficult in France), but can't help worrying about the many vacant faces she sees on the women sitting next to the sandbox in Paris's countless beautiful parks. And it was in Paris, where I saw myself how a mother rendered a public toilet unusable for all other people that day by holding her toddler several arm's lengths above the bowl and telling her to let it run. . . .

Leslie Kern, whose *Feminist City* I already mentioned, writes that the subservience of the modern mother is also true for Canada and the United States. A contemporary mom has to perform so many tasks and activities, which globalization has rendered almost universal: visiting the park, sitting at a café, shopping in stores selling books and expensive toys and clothes for mother and child, buying organic food in grocery stores, demanding new roads and houses, searching high and low for good schools, and so on.

Kern also addresses the "toilet discussion," which is a hot potato in feminist circles. She opts for a liberal argument that there have to be public toilets for *all* people, and diaper-changing tables in both men's and women's public restrooms.

Unfortunately, Kern can sometimes be condescending, for instance when (regarding menus) she offers this simple equation: more salads = more female customers. Well . . . she should be happy that many women tend to eat healthy food that doesn't involve the death of other living creatures.

Kern mentions poor female immigrants, who often work as nannies while their own kids are at home in Asia. This situation is popular in the Netherlands, where well-paid couples usually employ a woman from Indonesia to care for their children.

In times of instability, of postmodern fluctuation and insecurity, many people tend to stick to traditional values (like family) in order to find some kind of footing. It helps if you opt for mainstream concepts or in general a conservative lifestyle; there's comfort in following the crowd and sharing your set of beliefs with the like-minded.

Kern also thinks all women are the caring type, which is simply not true. In her opinion, there is some kind of general female virtue, which comes with the sex. In fact, it comes with the gender: there are women who reject care work, and also reject motherhood.

Yet many people become parents. Doing so has lots of advantages. If you are, say, forty, and you meet a new person at a party, one of the first questions you'll be asked is: *Do you have kids?* These are friendly, average people who mean no harm, and yet they cause it involuntarily. Not only might they hurt the feelings of the childless, but they perpetuate existing norms. Everyone who doesn't procreate is outside the norm. Some breeders really rub in their conviction that they are better people because they managed to reproduce. There's something in this concept that's hard to fathom. Why should the fact that you used your reproductive system make you more interesting, intelligent, or responsible? Unfortunately, you often observe quite the opposite.

There are countless examples of vibrant, pretty young women entering the workforce—and look at them after their first or second child! It's often so depressing you can only avert your eyes. It can't be helped that the female body will always show if it's given birth. There may also be many health complications, which are generally completely ignored by prospective fathers (it's not their body) and mothers (they want this baby, no matter what, and anyway, *those side effects are only going to happen to other women*).

One major problem is of course the social pressure that every *woman* has to deal with. Some males, too, tell stories about interfering relatives or friends; but it's usually the female who, because of her biological endowment, must bear the brunt of pro-natalist propaganda.

Some women don't want to feel left out if all their friends, relatives, neighbors, and colleagues "start a family." It is hard to tolerate if you're in a group of women who are all mothers—the topics are often so banal it's not easy to rid your mind of them. But it is possible to find childfree friends—maybe not in your workplace or even your village, but they're somewhere out there. For example, there are many Facebook groups and other forums for the childfree, which helps. There is an online network connecting those without kids.

A problem shared is a problem halved—well, many parents think so. They usually want to convert you, since there is no greater challenge than changing a convinced childfree person's mind. If people who once claimed to be childfree finally become parents, other breeders' gleeful smiles can't be ignored. *Got what they deserved at last; why should they have been so lucky?* they seem to say. But they weren't forced to reproduce; they chose this fate voluntarily, at least in most cases.

On the other hand, an article in the *New England Journal of Medicine* found that 45 percent of pregnancies in the United States were unplanned! (Finer & Zolna 2016). What happened to contraception? Health education? Abortion? It's absolutely crucial to support women (and men) who decide not to do what their "biology" and a pro-natalist society tell them to do. Contraceptive devices and safe abortions should be free and available for everyone who needs and wants them.

It's not only "the church" that's opposed to contraception and abortion, but (unfortunately) conservative parties and many other groups and individuals as well. We must encourage those who don't want to sit miserably with the other parents while their child performs in a crappy school play. So many unhappy couples could be saved! We need more childfree role models who show young people that their parents' decision wasn't necessarily the best, and that there *are* other brilliant options, especially if you want to avoid becoming like everybody else—a boring person living in the suburbs with a mortgage, two kids, enjoying one vacation per year in a family-friendly location.

History is full of childfree women who are still remembered and celebrated today because they achieved something bigger than just popping out babies. Jeanne d'Arc, for instance, could have stayed in her French village and become a mom like all the other peasant girls. Instead, she chose combat and became famous all over the world. Rosa Parks never had children, but every *German* child learns about her bus boycott.

Amelia Earhart is another favorite example of mine. Not only did she set many records as first female aviator, but she was a feminist. She supported other women immensely. Her encouraging words are one thing (she gave many talks and wrote several books about her adventures), but what's really impressive is her activism in the Ninety-Nines, an organization for female pilots. These alone would be more than enough to make her a role model, but she's also famous for her astonishing attitude toward marriage. Although she finally married George Putnam, who had to propose several times before she accepted him, she pointed out that faithfulness wasn't something to be expected from her nor him. She needed space and time for herself, otherwise she couldn't deal with the cage of their relationship, however pleasant the cage might be. These are genuinely feminist words! Nowadays they'd be less remarkable, but for the 1930s, those words are astonishing.

It's needless to point out that women like Earhart are childfree. If marriage is enough to make her feel trapped, what would the shackles of motherhood do to such a person? Earhart got along well with George's kids, but someone who loves their liberty and independence deeply rarely feels the need to procreate. It's a tragedy she disappeared so soon (aged thirty-nine) in 1937, when her plane disappeared in the Pacific Ocean. But Earhart said that death wasn't something she feared. She dreaded a dull, monotonous existence! And *that* she'd successfully avoided, and become famous along the way.

Inspiring other people can give you a feeling so exquisite it's hard to describe. You don't need your own museum like Amelia Earhart. If a young woman of sixteen writes you a long email to thank you from the bottom of her heart, that fills you with great joy too. This girl outlined how her philosophy teacher had shown his students an extract from my book and a video. She—like many women who contacted me—had never had the courage to admit that she didn't want to become a mother. Thanks to my work, she said, she was now proud of her decision and communicated it openly.

Bearing in mind that conservatives wanted me removed as a teacher, I found it courageous of the girl's teacher to use my content in class. I do have the occasional cool colleague! One lives in Berlin and invited me to talk in front of his philosophy class, as he considered it crucial they get to know what he called my "unique combination of radical feminism, ecologically responsible living, and anti-natalism."

If you think about what makes a good life, how you want to live it so it doesn't hurt anyone else (human or nonhuman), what makes sense and what doesn't? No matter if you approach this question philosophically, politically, ecologically, or from a feminist point of view, the result is always to refrain from procreation.

Molding yourself to pre-existing models isn't what life is about. Yes, every country has stupid old-fashioned advice about what you have to do: build a house, plant a tree, have a child. But sometimes the list isn't so banal. As one Ukrainian friend told me, their list featured killing at least one Russian!

Remaining childfree is no guarantee you'll become famous, of course, since not everyone can be an Amelia Earhart. But living independently and enjoying your life while making sure you don't harm anyone else is always very satisfying. One woman wrote to tell me she'd tried to live an ecofriendly life for decades but had simply missed the fact that her childfree lifestyle was her biggest contribution to the environment. Since realizing this, she's even happier with her choice and interestingly is more active in her vegan community too. She's gained lots of self-confidence, thereby also inspiring others.

Removing the scales from people's eyes can also be very rewarding. One older gentleman from Vienna told me about his decades of living childfree. However, he said, he'd been somewhat ashamed of his "lack of feeling." In conservative Austria, *he* was considered a freak because he didn't have the urge to father a child, and two girlfriends had left him because of it. In his soccer club, his teammates hadn't fully accepted him: yes, he played well; yes, he had a good job; and yes, he had a nice partner. But why didn't he make her pregnant? *What was he waiting for?*

The man began to feel desperate and excluded, especially when his partner finally moved out because she, too, didn't understand "what was wrong with him." Almost forty years later, he'd read about my work in the newspaper and it hit him: He'd always been an anti-natalist who just couldn't see why he should create another person. His emails were enormously touching.

It's hard for everyone who decides not to have children. Mainstream opinion and media are still absolutely pro-natalist, and they exert a lot of pressure. Commercials, for instance, favor pro-natalist attitudes (in newspapers, on TV, and on the internet; not to mention advertising billboards, newsstands near malls or bus stops, on the subway, at an airport, you name it). All these advertisements feature happy families. No wonder one woman who had killed her infant said family life was nothing like the ads on TV. Of course, this is a horrific and extreme case, but a general trend is evident: the media glorify family life. Plain and simple. Mothers are always happy and beautiful, and so are the dads with successful careers. (Sometimes, the mothers also work—but they don't have to.)

Even when the ad doesn't seem to promote a pro-natalist agenda, you find one cropping up. I've seen a spot about photography (and useful equipment for this hobby) that mentions important, great events that you can eternalize through it. You expect absolutely earth-shattering events of global significance. What do you see? A pregnant woman. Really?

Another TV ad starts like this: you see condoms, then the pill, then someone says surprise and you see the cutest baby in the world. This commercial is actually about financing your dream house, which you just have to buy if you want to *settle down*. Why do these conservative images hold such power?

But it's not only the world of those close to you (be it emotionally or otherwise) who apply that pressure. Cousins or friends seem to be engaging in some weird sort of competition over who can pop out more babies. That's why we have to encourage and empower women who don't want to participate!

Watch almost any movie and you'll see the myth of the happy family. Nor is it only rom-coms that end with the woman marrying the man of her dreams and *settling down* with him. Even *Star Wars* portrays parental love as the strongest force of all. Somehow, movies and novels fail to show how disastrous relationships between parents and children often are in real life. (Darth Vader would hardly be much of a role model as a father!) Some drama-documentaries feature abandoned kids or violent dads, but that's about it. And the message usually is that, yes, child abuse exists, but luckily, it's very rare.

Well, it's not. Many women (and some men) prostitute themselves later in life due to terrible sexual abuse they suffered as a child—mostly with their own fathers. The German therapist Ingeborg Kraus, who works with prostitutes and researches connections between trauma and prostitution, mentions this fact in all her articles and talks. Yet the myth of the happy sex worker doesn't die; nor does that of happy children and parents. Anti-natalists, of course, argue that such a tragic childhood is a possibility every new person faces, so it's always better not to reproduce.

5
PHILOSOPHY: ANTI-NATALISM

Pain, fatigue, disabilities, dysfunctions, accidents, wars, natural disasters, boredom, sadness, poverty, old age, distress, agony, loneliness, fear, and death—there are countless negative conditions that afflict mind and body, and the whole world. Everyone knows this, yet so many of us inflict this condition upon completely innocent new people, our children. One *always* harms creatures by bringing them into this world: this is the anti-natalist credo. If you really love them, don't have them.

Many philosophers have told us existence equals suffering. Sophocles and Euripides (ca. 480–406 BCE) were among the first to do so. Epicurus argued that children were thrown into agony and that death wasn't something to be afraid of, because it's not here as long as we are alive and, when it arrives, we're not here to notice it.

Heinrich Heine, the German poet, wrote many centuries later that sleep was good, and death even better, although none was as good as not having been born at all. Schopenhauer, already mentioned because of his strong animal advocacy (cf. Chapter 2), pointed out in one of his essays that life is a kind of disturbing episode that interrupts the calmness of non-existence. Gustav Flaubert, who "invented" the *flâneur*, wrote in one of his letters that he shuddered when he so much as thought of procreation. French philosopher Michel de Montaigne argued that one shouldn't cry when somebody dies but when they are born. This is anti-natalism in the sixteenth century. You could say that life is a sexually transmitted disease with a mortality rate of one hundred percent.

The most prominent contemporary scholar is David Benatar, who teaches philosophy at the University of Cape Town. He argues that it can never be morally acceptable to produce any affliction, so there should be zero reproduction. In his own words: "Since all existers suffer harm, procreation always causes harm (Benatar 2007, p. 50)."

Many people can't believe anyone really believes this. They're usually outraged and their worst fear seems to be that, at some point in time, there might not be any human beings anymore on this planet. Of course, this *will* happen when Earth becomes uninhabitable, either due to our own behavior or the sun's expansion. But merely picturing a world without humans seems to be a horrifying scenario for many of us. Are people so brilliant that there have to be billions of us? Benatar adds: "[T]he concern that humans will not exist at some future time is either a symptom of the human arrogance that our presence makes the world a better place or is some misplaced sentimentalism (ibid., p. 200)."

Janosch, the famous German artist who invented the "tabby duck" featured in several children's books, is another well-known childfree anti-natalist. He argues that out of a thousand people only one leads a life without major tribulations. The other 999 suffer, whether from illness of mind or body, lack of adequate housing or employment, having no satisfying relationship(s), and so on. Benatar echoes this on the first page of his formidable book: "The quality of even the best lives is very bad—and considerably worse than most people recognize it to be."

In response to the above observation, people usually proclaim incredulously that their lives are fantastic and the pain is negligible. Is it? Psychology proves that we all have a certain optimism when assessing the quality of our lives. The Pollyanna Principle entails, as Benatar puts it, the "inclination to recall positive rather than negative experiences" (ibid., pp. 64–65). Indeed, many people think their lives are better than average.

How does this happen? Benatar mentions three phenomena: adaptation, accommodation, and habituation. In the first case, you can always adjust your expectations, if your life gets worse. Benatar tells us that many people insist on their good quality of life, and the satisfaction they receive every day, even though there's always a lot of dissatisfaction. He lists negative experiences many people have to face on a daily basis: natural disasters, hunger, war, rape, poverty, and violence among them, and stresses that procreation resembles Russian roulette: *your* child could be ill, raped, or murdered. What they *definitely* have to face is death. Life is always a preparation for death. Why should we put someone in the situation of having to learn to die?

Let's remember there are empirical asymmetries between wonderful and horrible events, objects, and feelings. Atrocious pain is worse than perfect bliss is good. Being tortured will make more of an impression on you than a few seconds of total happiness. Pain in general lasts longer than pleasure.

Parents feel proud because they "bestow" life. But such a "gift" happens without any regard for the recipient's inability to accept it, since they wouldn't exist without it and never had a chance to reject it. Creating a new person under these circumstances is an act of caprice (to put it mildly): the creature is always thrown into life and condemned to live it. Every life starts with a violation of the newborn's will!

Furthermore, if bearing children is about the gift of life, you can always adopt or foster the millions of children without families and therefore do some real good. But strangely, most parents want their own mini-me. . . . When we give up on having kids, we cede a highly dubious personal satisfaction to prevent great suffering; conversely, uttering the same empty clichés and breeding as normal gets us nowhere. Yet if you say that breeders are selfish, or point out that, in 2019, 4,140 kids in England were waiting to be adopted (these numbers were released by the Adoption and Special Guardianship Leadership Board), whereas only 1,700 families considered adopting a suitable child, you're attacked. It's vital to encourage more people to adopt. Why not use financial incentives too?

But, as we've seen, education, the mass media, and economic and legal policy all favor pro-natalism and encourage people to have children—instead of discouraging them, which would be highly beneficial for all involved. Women and men who refuse to procreate are considered a threat to capitalism, so the state will never encourage them. New books for German grammar school students neglect risks of pregnancy and childbirth, while the authors of a brand-new pupils' biology book emphasize the joy of both and portray them as some kind of great magic power that women possess. Yes, women experience their period once a month but *to make up for that* they have the great capability of giving life. Such language sounds as if Catholic priests had written it decades ago! But no outrage here, which fits our current backlash perfectly. Very young women are thus molded the way our patriarchal society wants them to be: docile breeders who are proud of owning ovaries.

TV shows like *Kleines Wunder—großes Glück* (*Small Miracle—Great Happiness*) are popping up. Kleines Wunder is a whole series devoted to the biological process of pregnancy and delivery. Often, you see how hard and dangerous it is for mother and infant, yet it's always "worth it" because you have a new human being who completely depends on you. . . . Twenty years ago, there were no series like this (which is only one of many), which clearly shows how severe the backlash is nowadays. The religiously charged word *miracle* is provocation enough, if you take into account that a miracle is by definition an extremely rare occurrence, and yet there are currently more than seven billion miracles roaming the earth.

Yet there are new products every day, because parents are important as consumers first and foremost, although politicians tell them otherwise on a regular and hypocritical basis. Wunderkinder, for instance, is a kind of countdown box for pregnant women with small (useless) surprises for either mom or baby for each day of the pregnancy. I'll agree that women who have a difficult pregnancy and aren't allowed to do anything might be cheered up by such a box. But why the presumptuous name? Isn't it enough anymore to bear a child; does it have to be a prodigy? And why buy so many superfluous things even before the baby arrives? There are countries where parents don't have any such luxury goods.

French philosopher Michel Onfray, who emphasizes that it's downright cruel to condemn children to work, obedience, frustration, and submission, points out in *Théorie du corps amoureux* (*Theory of the Loving Body*) (2000) that there isn't much love in transmitting this vileness to the body from our own. Théophile de Giraud, another philosopher writing in French, is quite famous for his brilliant texts about anti-natalism. The Belgian published *L'art de guillotiner les procréateurs: Manifeste anti-nataliste* (*The Art of Guillotining Procreators: An Anti-Natalist Manifesto*) in 2006 and continues to advocate this philosophy.

As long ago as 1925, Virginia Woolf already had it right: this world is not one to bring children into. One always perpetuates suffering. This is one of the messages of her novel *Mrs. Dalloway*. Woolf was a pioneer in the very early beginnings of the polyamory movement, having a tolerant husband who didn't mind her affairs with women.

Eugène Ionesco, author of *Rhinoceros and Other Plays*, prominently focuses on the absurdity of this life, the span between a horrible birth and a death he was equally afraid of. The time in between wasn't something positive for him, either. (The Austrian dramatist Thomas Bernhard shared this attitude wholeheartedly). Leo Tolstoy, the great Russian novelist, also called life a stupid and a spiteful joke someone had played on him.

Marie Huot (1846–1930), a French poet, writer, feminist, and animal rights activist (funny how these attitudes seem to go together so often throughout history), pointed out how cruel it was to procreate, as giving life always means giving death as well. Of course, not giving life would lead to the end of humanity, and she was cool enough to admit she had no problem with that.

Philosophers have also thought this way. David Benatar points out that the *human condition* is more accurately described as the *human predicament* (in his book with the very same title). Amelioration of some degree is sometimes possible, but he calls this the existential equivalent of palliative care (p. 6). Benatar talks about reproduction as the creation of new milltreaders, which is absolutely correct. This phenomenon is intergenerational; we are all on the long, repetitive journey to nowhere.

Thomas Metzinger, a German professor of theoretical philosophy, hypothesizes a benevolent superintelligence, which would also conclude that non-existence is in the best interest of all future self-aware beings in our world. Biological creatures aren't able to realize this fact because they are subject to their existence bias.

To conclude: If you want to prevent suffering and death, prevent birth. If you suffered in life and want others to suffer as you did because "you turned out fine"—well, you did not, in fact, turn out fine. Overdose and suicide rates climb, but never mind: Let other people's kids kill themselves. The optimism of most parents is quite astonishing, more so as the situation our world is in continues to deteriorate. As long as there are people like Björn Vedder, a German author with whom I share a publishing house, who tells his readers that fatherhood is great and promises you a wonderful life, business will go on as usual. Breeders need little encouragement anyway.

It's quite astonishing that so many *serious* writers realize that life isn't as great as self-help books, trashy novelists, and other people who own a computer—to say nothing of movie makers or advertisers—keep telling us. Feel-good literature is very popular.

What harm does one child do, mothers and fathers often ask. Well, every single parent considers their child wonderful and perfect and someone whom everyone else should indulge. But it's never just *one* child or *one* set of parents: there are billions more who think that way. One particular child is never the problem, multiplying that by millions *is*.

If everyone had fewer children, everyone would benefit, and it wouldn't be discriminatory at all. If more money was available from fewer expenses on childcare, maternity leave, child tax credits, etc., we could genuinely combat poverty and diseases, improve infrastructure, and provide a better life for those who already exist. Medical institutions could focus on the important issues (and IVF is definitely not one of them) to make life better for the sick.

This moderate position—a voluntary one-child policy, easy access to birth control and sterilization, or perhaps sanctions on children beyond replacement level—doesn't satisfy some. C.S. Mireille from Ohio, for instance, is an author who argues for total abstinence from childbearing, and adoption for all those who have the incredible urge to parent. She correctly points out that idolizing personal freedom has led us all into our current ecological predicament.

As I've discussed, such ideas are considered taboo. In Germany, a headline like *How many children is too many?* would never be allowed. Hypocrisy and cowardice rule supreme, reflected in the absence of phrases such as "replacement level" in our media. This is a function of German hubris and resurgent nationalism, both of which we should be ashamed of.

In *One Child: Do We Have a Right to More?* Sarah Conly writes that having *several* children is a strain on the environment that ethically conscious people shouldn't consider any more. It's obvious that birth strikers are no nihilists (although it's quite popular to refer to them as such); far from it, they are driven by a powerful sense of meaning and purpose. No wonder they promote co-parenting and other modern, innovative concepts for those who really love kids and not only their own genes.

In her article "Why Choosing to Have Children is an Ethical Issue," and her book *Why Have Children? The Ethical Debate*, Christine Overall, a Canadian feminist philosopher, debunks the popular myths about childbearing: it's neither natural nor a great gift. These two powerful narratives remain omnipresent in our everyday life.

You can never ask the unborn's opinion; you always bring them into existence without their approval. Yes, we go through this life because we have to; but does that give us the right to put another person through the same grind? This is how society works, but does that mean we have to continue these established practices without challenging them? We are mindful, rational beings, so let's start acting accordingly.

In 2019, an Indian man sued his parents' for having done exactly this (Pandey 2019). So, not *everyone* is happy about the so-called gift of life. And it's not about the child, anyway. As Benatar observes, reproduction is first and foremost about the parents: "Making babies for the tribe, the nation, or state earns one some status. But it is the procreative and related interests, I suspect, that account for most of the intentional baby-making. Parents satisfy biological desires [. . .]. Progenies provide parents with some form of immortality" (p. 98).

No wonder there are extreme anti-natalists who claim that parents are murderers because they produce a new person who will definitely die. They don't care, as long as they live on. They won't be here to watch this, will they? Well, some are continuing their lives, and of course this is a tragedy; but nevertheless, as Benatar puts it, every birth is a death in waiting. "Sandwiched between birth and death is a struggle for meaning and a desperate attempt to ward off life's suffering" (p. 207).

Do the childbearing never wonder how hard it is to see your mother lying in a hospital bed? My mom died when she was sixty, and it was indescribably painful as a thirty-something woman to watch her fade away in only three weeks. She was bouncing around in January and in February she was dead. Heinrich Heine couldn't help us; no "Dann steig ich gewaffnet hervor aus dem Grab (Then I shall rise again from my grave in full armor)" for my mom. She's gone for good and the shock took me ages to recover from.

For most of us, burying our parents is usually a shattering task (although some may rejoice); parents who have to bury their child often never fully recover (if at all). Yet both happen, as does the fact that everyone in the U.K. has a fifty percent chance of getting cancer. If people imposed a one-in-two risk on someone else in a context that wasn't reproduction, nobody would applaud. So why those completely different standards if the issue is procreation?

Another different standard without any good reason is the fact that no other species causes so much pain and suffering, murders so many animals, or destroys so much of the natural world, and yet we don't think it's wrong to breed more and more new members of this species. Why do humans add 3,500 lives every twenty minutes, while losing one or more species in the same span of time?

Some of you reading this may feel that I'm blaming you for having to watch your parents die. Of course not! It's your parents' fault for bringing you into the world. They forced life upon you; they can't expect you to be eternally grateful. If you're someone considering becoming a parent, why would you want to inflict upon a child such horrors? One in five of us will die of cardiovascular disease or cancer. If we breed, we inflict this fate upon others and make them watch when it's our turn. So, as Benatar states, it only makes sense that "there is a (moral) duty not to procreate" (p. 14). Plain and simple.

As we've seen, every "democracy has an inherent bias towards pro-natalism" (ibid. p. 11), and as Benatar argues, this stance is directly related to the fact that every "democracy favors breeding over immigration" (ibid.). Yet what will we do when millions of climate refugees from Africa and Asia start to arrive in the West. Fascist states will want to keep them out, although it's their fault that many regions in the developing world won't be habitable anymore.

And it's not just humans who will flee climate change. Polar bears are now being forced to enter populated areas in their search for food. As the sea ice melts, the glaciers retreat, and the snowpacks thin, a quarter of the planet's human population will face water shortages. A new international study blames global heating and rising demand (Watts 2019).

Everywhere we look, the sheer numbers of humans cause destruction and death. On November 28, 2019, a young dead sperm whale was washed up on an island in Scotland with 220 pounds (!) of trash in its stomach. The rubbish included plastic cups, bags, packing straps, tubing, rope, net, and gloves. And still we add ever more plastic consumers!

Why is this climate change called human-made? Because we—an arrogant, greedy species on two legs—can't help existing. Why can't we refrain from actively, consciously producing someone new, someone with no choice but to pollute the environment even more, someone who would contribute to species extinction, glacier melting, extreme weather conditions, floods, fires, storms, and so on? And what would we bequeath these new consumers? Contaminated oceans and rivers full of plastic and chemical poisons; an agriculture that won't be sustainable anymore; sewage pollution and farm runoff leading our oceans to suffer.

Every day you find new reports showing how wrecked our planet is: oceans losing oxygen because of climate change; more and bigger "dead zones"; rising sea levels threatening to flood London. Around the world, major infrastructure is at risk, and many cities on the coast face a bleak prospect.

When resource limits are exceeded, starvation, predation, and disease will limit our population growth. We can still prevent these catastrophes from happening, if we're lucky—and if we stop breeding. So, what are our priorities? Do we want to continue consuming, or do we want to save the ecosystems upon which all life, including our own, depends? If we continuously degrade our ecosystems through desertification, deforestation, pollution, and destruction of biodiversity, all productivity will decrease, which will only place more strain on those ecosystems. Humanity is likely to need eighty percent more food in 2100 than now. This isn't only because of a growing population (contributing sixty percent) but, as a study published in *PLOS One* found, also due to a greater calorie requirement, as humans become taller and larger! (Depenbusch & Klasen 2019).

"If we take a cold, hard look at the human condition," concludes David Benatar, "we see an unpleasant picture. However, there are powerful biological drives against fully recognizing the awfulness of the human predicament that explain why so many people succeed in putting it out of their minds for much of the time. This is a mixed blessing. Ignorance is an existential analgesic, but those who do not sufficiently feel the weight of the human predicament are also vectors for its transmission to new generations" (p. 214).

Some optimists claim that anti-natalism is becoming the new veganism—well, definitely not in Germany. It should become exactly that, of course; of that there's absolutely no doubt. But it's much harder to promote. Let's hope that at least some inhabitants of the West are conscious of their responsibility for animals and people in poorer countries and act accordingly. It's crucial for the survival of us all.

BIBLIOGRAPHY

Adams, C. (1990). *The Sexual Politics of Meat: A Feminist-Vegetarian Critical Theory* (London, UK: Continuum).

Anapol, D. (2012). *Polyamory in the Twenty-first Century: Love and Intimacy with Multiple Partners* (Lanham, MD: Rowman & Littlefield).

———. (2005) *Compersion: Meditations on Using Jealousy as a Path to Unconditional Love* (e-book self-published).

Anonymous (2019). A Letter to . . . Our Neighbours with a Baby," November 16, https://www.theguardian.com/lifeandstyle/2019/nov/16/a-letter-to-our-neighbours-with-a-baby.

Arndt, S. (2020). *Sexismus: Geschichte einer Unterdrückung* [*Sexism: History of an Oppression*] (Munich, Germany: C.H. Beck).

Backes, G. & Clemens, W. (2013). *Lebensphase Alter: Eine Einführung in die sozialwissenschaftliche Alternsforschung* [*The Aging Period of Life: An Introduction to Social Science Research on Aging*] (Weinheim, Germany: Juventa Verlag GmbH).

Baker (2019). Number of Pregnancies Can Increase Risk of Heart Failure Later in Life—Herald Sun. Baker Heart & Diabetes Institute, August 14, https://baker.edu.au/news/in-the-media/pregnancy-heart-risk.

Barthes, R. (1977/1979). *Fragments d'un discours amoureux. A Lover's Discourse: Fragments* (New York, NY: Farrar, Straus and Giroux).

Benatar, D. (2007). *Better Never to Have Been: The Harm of Coming into Existence* (New York, NY: Oxford University Press).

Benatar, D. (2017). *The Human Predicament: A Candid Guide to Life's Biggest Questions* (New York, NY: Oxford University Press).

Blackstone, A. (2014). Childless . . . or Childfree? *Journal of Health and Social Behavior* 13(4): 68–70, https://doi.org/10.1177/1536504214558221.

Brun, M. (2018). *Brigitte Macron: L'affranchie* [Brigitte Macron: The Freed] (Nanterre, France: L'Archipel).

Bytheway, B. (1995). *Ageism*. (Maidenhead, UK: Open University Press).

Cain, S. (2019). Women Are Happier Without Children or a Spouse, Says Happiness Expert. *The Observer*, May 25, https://www.theguardian.com/lifeandstyle/2019/may/25/women-happier-without-children-or-a-spouse-happiness-expert.

Casey, K. (2019). Why Climate Change Is an Irrelevance, Economic Growth Is a Myth and Sustainability Is Forty Years Too Late. *Global Comment*, November 20, https://globalcomment.com/why-climate-change-is-an-irrelevance-economic-growth-is-a-myth-and-sustainability-is-forty-years-too-late/.

Chalker, R. (2000). *The Clitoral Truth: The Secret World at Your Fingertips* (New York, NY: Seven Stories Press).

Chattopadhay, S. (2012). The Birth of a Male Contraceptive. Open, April 1, https://openthemagazine.com/features/living/the-birth-of-a-male-contraceptive.

Conly, S. (2015). *One Child: Do We Have a Right to More?* (Oxford: Oxford University Press).

Connolly K. & Taylor, M. (2019). Extinction Rebellion Founder's Holocaust Remarks Spark Fury. *The Guardian*, November 20, https://www.theguardian.com/environment/2019/nov/20/extinction-rebellion-founders-holocaust-remarks-spark-fury.

Crenshaw, K. (2014). *On Intersectionality: The Essential Writings of Kimberlé Crenshaw* (New York, NY: New Press).

Dann, C. (1979). *The Animals of Farthing Wood* (London: Hutchinson).

Depenbusch, L. & Klasen, S. (2019). The Effect of Bigger Human Bodies on the Future Global Calorie Requirements. *PLOS One*, December 4, https://doi.org/10.1371/journal.pone.0223188.

Delany, S. (1999). *Times Square Red, Times Square Blue* (New York: New York University Press).

De Giraud, T. (2006). *L'art de guillotiner les procréateurs: Manifeste anti-nataliste* [The Art of Guillotining Procreators: Anti-natalist Manifesto] (Nancy, France: Le Mort-Qui-Trompe).

DePaulo, B. (2007). *Singled Out: How Singles Are Stereotyped, Stigmatized, and Ignored, and Still Live Happily Ever After* (New York, NY: St. Martin's Press).

Dickinson, K. (2018). Decades of Data Suggest Parenthood Makes People Unhappy. *Big Think*, December 17, https://bigthink.com/the-present/should-you-have-kids.

Dolan, P. (2019). *Happy Ever After: Escaping the Myth of the Perfect Life* (London, UK: Penguin Books).

Donath, O. (2017). *Regretting Motherhood: A Study* (Berkeley, CA: North Atlantic Books).

Faludi, S. (1992). *Backlash: The Undeclared War Against American Women* (New York, NY: Doubleday).

Farley, M. (2009). Myths & Facts About Legalized Prostitution. *Prostitution Research & Education*, https://prostitutionresearch.com/myths-facts-about-legalized-prostitution-3.

Finer L. & Zolna M. (2016). Declines in Unintended Pregnancy in the United States, 2008–2011. New England Journal of Medicine 374(9): 843–852, https://www.doi.org/10.1056/NEJMsa1506575.

Fitzgerald, M. (2019). Climate Change Is a Feminist Issue. *Our World*, October 27, https://ourworld.unu.edu/en/climate-change-is-a-feminist-issue.

Fitzsimmons, C. (2019). "It Doesn't Feel Justifiable": The Couples Not Having Children Because of Climate Change. *Sydney Morning*

Herald, September 22, https://www.smh.com.au/lifestyle/life-and-relationships/it-doesn-t-feel-justifiable-the-couples-not-having-children-because-of-climate-change-20190913-p52qxu.html.

Fontanel, S. (2017). *Une Apparition*. (Paris: Robert Laffont).

Ford, L. (2019). UK Promises Extra £600m for Family Planning in Poorest Countries. *Guardian*, September 24, https://www.theguardian.com/global-development/2019/sep/24/uk-promises-extra-600m-family-planning-poorest-countries.

Franzen, J. (2019). What If We Stopped Pretending? *The New Yorker*, September 8, https://www.newyorker.com/culture/cultural-comment/what-if-we-stopped-pretending.

Götmark, F. & Maynard, R. (2019). The World and the UN Must Reduce Population Growth. *Project Syndicate*, September 10, https://www.project-syndicate.org/commentary/new-sdg-dampen-population-growth-by-frank-gotmark-and-robin-maynard-2019-09.

Greer, G. (1993). *The Change* (New York, NY: Ballantine Books).

Griffiths, S. The Effect of Childbirth No-one Talks About. *BBC News*, April 24, https://www.bbc.com/future/article/20190424-the-hidden-trauma-of-childbirth.

Grosz, E. & Probyn, E. (eds.) (1995). *Sexy Bodies: The Strange Carnalities of Feminism* (New York, NY: Routledge).

Harmange, P. (2020). *I Hate Men*. (Lehrer, N., Trans.) (London, UK: HarperCollins).

Healthyway (2017). 14 Ways Your Body Will Never Be the Same After You Have a Baby. February 10, https://www.healthyway.com/content/ways-your-body-will-never-be-the-same-after-you-have-a-baby.

Javelosa, J. (2016). David Attenborough: If We Don't Limit Our Population Growth, the Natural World Will. Futurism, December 19, https://futurism.com/david-attenborough-if-we-dont-limit-our-population-growth-the-natural-world-will.

Jeffreys, S. (2020). *Trigger Warning: My Lesbian Feminist Life* (Australia: Spinifex Press).

Johnson, M. (2016). Want to Save Your Marriage? Don't Have Kids. *The Guardian*, May 24, https://www.theguardian.com/commentisfree/2016/may/24/marriage-kids-children-relationship-suffers-research.

Kemmerer, L. (ed.) (2011). *Sister Species: Women, Animals and Social Justice* (Champaign, IL: University of Illinois Press).

Kern, L. (2019). *Feminist City: A Field Guide* (Chico, CA: Between the Lines).

Klein, R. (2017). *Surrogacy: A Human Rights Violation* (North Geelong, Australia: Spinifex Press).

Kobek, J. (2019). *Only Americans Burn in Hell* (Los Angeles: We Heard You Like Books).

Korsgaard, C. (2018). *Fellow Creatures: Our Obligations to the Other Animals* (Oxford, UK: Oxford University Press).

Kreamer, A. (2014). *Going Gray: What I Learned About Beauty, Sex, Work, Motherhood, Authenticity, and Everything Else That Really Matters* (New York: Hachette Book Group).

Langdon, B. (2019). If We Want to Stop the Climate Emergency, We Need to Break the Taboo Around Population and Contraception. The Independent, November 7, https://www.independent.co.uk/voices/population-taboo-equality-climate-emergency-contraception-a9189386.html.

Latour, B. (2007). *Reassembling the Social: An Introduction to Actor-Network-Theory* (Oxford: Oxford University Press).

Ley, D. (2012). *Insatiable Wives: Women Who Stray and the Men Who Love Them* (Lanham, MD: Rowman & Littlefield).

Maxton, G. & Randers, J. (2016). *Reinventing Prosperity: Managing Economic Growth to Reduce Unemployment, Inequality, and Climate Change* (Rome: Club of Rome).

McGrath, M. (2019). Climate Change: 12 Years to Save the Planet? Make That 18 Months. *BBC News*, July 24, https://www.bbc.com/news/science-environment-48964736.

Mika, B. (2017). *Die Feigheit der Frauen* [The Cowardice of Women] (Gütersloh, Germany: Bertelsmann Verlag).

Moran, C. (2016). *How to Be a Woman* (New York, NY: HarperCollins).

Mundlos, C. (2012). *Mütterterror: Angst, Neid und Aggressionen unter Müttern* [Maternal Terror: Fear, Envy, and Aggression Among Mothers] (Antwerpen, Belgium: Tectum).

MacCormack, P. (2020). *The Ahuman Manifesto: Activism for the End of the Anthropocene* (London, UK: Bloomsbury Academic).

Murphy, M. (2019). No, I Will Not Listen to the Children. *The Spectator*, September 30, https://spectatorworld.com/topic/listen-children-climate-change.

North, A. (2019). Joe Biden Hasn't Changed His Behavior with Girls and Women. For His Base, That Might Be Fine. *Vox*, June 15, https://www.vox.com/Joe   2019/6/13/18663399/joe-biden-10-year-old-hyde-women.

Onfray, M. (2000). *Théorie du corps amoureux* [Theory of the amorous body] (Paris, France: Éditions Grasset).

Open University (2013). Enduring Love? Couple Relationships in the 21st Century, https://www.open.ac.uk/researchprojects/enduringlove.

Overall, C. (n.d.). Why Choosing to Have Children Is an Ethical Choice. The MIT Press Reader, https://thereader.mitpress.mit.edu/choosing-children-ethical-issue.

———. (2013). *Why Have Children? The Ethical Debate* (Cambridge, MA: MIT Press).

Pandey,G. (2019). Indian Man to Sue Parents for Giving Birth to Him. *BBC News*, February 7,   https://www.bbc.com/news/world-asia-india-47154287.

Pearson, C. (2019). Study Finds What Parents Know: They Don't Sleep Well for Baby's First 6 Years. *Huffpost*, March 5, https://www.huffpost.com/entry/study-parents-sleep-babies_l_5c7d8187e4b0129e36bdbd75.

Peck, E. (1971). *The Baby Trap* (New York: Bernard Geis Associates).

Pelluchon, C. (2017). *Manifeste animaliste: Politiser la cause animale* [Animalist Manifesto: Politicizing the Animal Cause] (Paris, France: Alma Éditeur).

Rauch, J. (2017). EMMA, February, https://www.emma.de/authors/judith-rauch.

Raymond, J. (1993). *Women as Wombs: Reproductive Technologies and the Battle Over Women's Freedom* (San Francisco, CA: HarperSanFrancisco).

Reinhardt, É. (2020). *Comédies françaises: roman* [French Comedies: A Novel] (Paris, France: Gallimard).

Ripple, W., Wolf, C., Newsome, T., et al. (2020). World Scientists' Warning of a Climate Emergency. BioScience 70(1): 8–12, https://doi.org/10.1093/biosci/biz088.

Rohy, V. (2000). *Impossible Women: Lesbian Figures and American Literature* (Ithaca, NY: Cornell University Press).

Sassin, W., Donskikh, O., Komissarov, S., et al. (2018). *Evolutionary Environments: Homo Sapiens—an Endangered Species?* (Innsbruck, Austria: Studia Universitätsverlag). The translations are mine.

Schellnhuber, H. (2015). *Selbstverbrennung: Die fatale Dreiecksbeziehung zwischen Klima, Mensch und Kohlenstoff* [Self-immolation: Fatal Relationship between Climate, Humans, and Carbon] (Gütersloh, Germany: Bertelsmann).

Siler, W. (2019). I Got a Vasectomy Because of Climate Change. *Outside Online*, November 21, https://www.outsideonline.com/culture/opinion/vasectomy-climate-change.

Solnit, R. (2020). *Recollections of My Nonexistence* (New York, NY: Viking Press).

Story, B. (2013). In/Different Cities: A Case for Contact at the Margins. *Social & Cultural Geography* 14(7): 752–761, https://doi.org/10.1080/14649365.2013.771209.

Sturges, F. (2020). Is *My Dark Vanessa* the Most Controversial Novel of the Year? Author Kate Elizabeth Russell Speaks Out. *The Guardian*,

March 13, https://www.theguardian.com/books/2020/mar/13/kate-elizabeth-russell-my-dark-vanessa-interview.

Televisor Troika (n.d.) Regretting Motherhood: A Documentary Film by Kristina Schippling, https://www.televisor.de/portfolio/regretting-motherhood.

Thomson, K. (2016). Kelvin Thomson SPA AGM 2016, https://population.org.au/video/kelvin-thomson-spa-agm-2016/.

Toepfer, R. (2020). *Kinderlosigkeit: Ersehnte, verweigerte und bereute Elternschaft im Mittelalter* [*Childlessness: Longed for, Refused, and Repented—Parenthood in the Middle Ages*] (Stuttgart, Germany: J.B. Metzler).

Turner, A. (2019). In Praise of Demographic Decline. *Project Syndicate*, July 2, https://www.project-syndicate.org/commentary/automation-favors-shrinking-populations-by-adair-turner-2019-07.

UNEP (2020). As Daily COVID-19 Cases Reach a New High, New Report Examines How to Prevent Future Pandemics, July 6, https://www.unep.org/news-and-stories/story/daily-covid-19-cases-reach-new-high-new-report-examines-how-prevent-future.

Wallace-Wells, D. (2019). *The Uninhabitable Earth: Life After Warming* (New York, NY: Random House).

Chan L. & Westoff, C (2010). Tubal Sterilization in the United States. *Fertility and Sterility* 94(1) June, https://www.fertstert.org/article/S0015-0282(10)00466-8/pdf.

Watts (2019). 1.9 Billion People at Risk from Mountain Water Shortages, Study Shows. *The Guardian*, December 9, https://www.theguardian.com/environment/2019/dec/09/billion-people-risk-water-supply-rising-demand-global-heating-mountain-ecosystem.

Wintour, P. (2019). Niger's President Blames Explosive Birth Rate on "A Misreading of Islam." *Guardian*, October 17, https://www.theguardian.com/global-development/2019/oct/17/nigers-president-blames-explosive-birth-rate-on-a-misreading-of-islam.

Wolf, N. (1990). *The Beauty Myth: How Images of Beauty Are Used Against Women* (New York, NY: Vintage Canada).

ABOUT THE AUTHOR

Photo credit: Juliane Zitzlsperger

Verena Brunschweiger is an author, passionate childfree activist, and feminist. She was born in Passau, Germany, in 1980. She studied German, English, and Philosophy at Regensburg University, receiving her PhD in 2007 and teaches at a Bavarian grammar school. She is a most passionate member of Theater Regensburg's extra choir, performing in several operas by Verdi, Wagner, and Bizet. She still accompanies her favorite professional basso on the piano. Reading books in any of the five languages she speaks is another great passion of hers.

About the Publisher

Lantern Publishing & Media was founded in 2020 to follow and expand on the legacy of Lantern Books—a publishing company started in 1999 on the principles of living with a greater depth and commitment to the preservation of the natural world. Like its predecessor, Lantern Publishing & Media produces books on animal advocacy, veganism, religion, social justice, humane education, psychology, family therapy, and recovery. Lantern is dedicated to printing in the United States on recycled paper and saving resources in our day-to-day operations. Our titles are also available as eBooks and audiobooks.

To catch up on Lantern's publishing program, visit us at www.lanternpm.org.

   facebook.com/lanternpm
twitter.com/lanternpm
instagram.com/lanternpm